PRAISE FOR
A Girl Named Zippy

"While reading *A Girl Named Zippy*, I started to dog-ear each page that contained a charming anecdote, a garden-fresh metaphor, a characterization shrewd as those from *Spoon River,* or a madeleine substitute worthy of Proust. My copy soon came to resemble a cone. *A Girl Named Zippy* seems to be just about the cleverest little memoir ever. I've told every friend I own to get a copy, and I find myself suddenly frantic to make new friends."

—*New York Newsday*

"It's a cliché to say that a good memoir reads like a well-crafted work of fiction, but Kimmel's smooth, impeccably humorous prose evokes her childhood as vividly as any novel. The truths of childhood are rendered in lush, yet simple prose. Dreamy and comforting, spiced with flashes of wit."   —*Publishers Weekly*

"Filled with good humor, fine storytelling, and acute observations of small-town life."   —*Library Journal*

"Nicknamed for her tendency to bolt around the house, Zippy is a spunky little girl trying to puzzle through the adult world (otherwise known as 1960s Mooreland, Ind.) in this gentle memoir."

—*People* magazine

"Fresh, funny, delightful, and very amusing."

—*Kirkus Reviews*

"Phenomenal. This is just perfectly written and right on target and she doesn't miss a beat."

—Kaye Gibbons, author of *Ellen Foster* and *A Virtuous Woman*

"A rarity: an original book, the freshest, most compelling child's voice since Ellen Foster. Hysterical, sometimes wrenching, Mooreland, Indiana, is filled with revelations. Haven Kimmel is a writer of genius who has penned a lovely poem to her heartland hometown."

—Lee Smith, author of *Oral History* and *Family Linen*

"The prose in this book is lovely and wise and sings as beautifully as 'Somewhere Over the Rainbow,' but written by Dorothy's wild, irreverent sister, the one you never saw in the movie who locked Dorothy outside with the tornado, sold Toto, set fire to the scarecrow, ate the flying monkeys, and painted all the blacktop roads in Mooreland, Indiana, the colors of the rainbow, the colors of imagination and heart and laughter."

—Lawrence Naumoff, author of *Rootie Kazootie* and *Silk Hope, NC*

"Sly, evocative, gentle, wry, and dead-on funny. Haven Kimmel is perfect on the details and spins graceful stories that sink in and stay with you for a good long time. This is, simply put, a masterful piece of writing—imagine pouring a highball, settling into a comfortable seat, and being entertained on a summer porch by a charming old friend."

—Martin Clark, author of *The Many Aspects of Mobile Home Living*

A Girl Named

ZIPPY

Also by Haven Kimmel

The Solace of Leaving Early

Broadway Books

NEW YORK

A Girl Named

ZIPPY

Growing

Up Small

in Mooreland,

Indiana

Haven Kimmel

Broadway Books titles may be purchased for business or promotional use or
for special sales. For information, please write to: Special Markets
Department, Random House, Inc., 1540 Broadway, New York, NY 10036.

PRINTED IN THE UNITED STATES OF AMERICA

BROADWAY BOOKS and its logo, a letter B bisected on the diagonal,
are trademarks of Broadway Books, a division of Random House, Inc.

Visit our website at www.broadwaybooks.com

First Broadway Books trade paperback edition published 2002

Designed by Nicola Ferguson

"Preface to a Twenty Volume Suicide Note" from the book
The LeRoi Jones/Amiri Baraka Reader by Amiri Baraka.
Copyright © 1991 by Amiri Baraka.
Appears by permission of the publisher, Thunder's Mouth Press.

Grateful acknowledgment is made to Carol Hoopingarner for the
photographs appearing on pages 1, 167, and 201.

The Library of Congress has cataloged the hardcover as follows:

Kimmel, Haven, 1965–
A girl named Zippy: growing up small in Mooreland, Indiana /
by Haven Kimmel.—1st ed.
p.   cm.
1. Kimmel, Haven, 1965—Childhood and youth.   2. Mooreland (Ind.)—
Biography.   3. Mooreland (Ind.)—Social life and customs—20th
century.   4. Girls—Indiana—Mooreland—Biography.
5. City and town life—Indiana—Mooreland.   I. Title.
F534.M675 K56 2001
977.2'64—dc21
00-027922

ISBN 0-7679-1505-4

5   7   9   10   8   6   4

For my mother
and
my sister

For absent friends

CONTENTS

A Girl Named

ZIPPY

PROLOGUE

If you look at an atlas of the United States, one published around, say, 1940, there is, in the state of Indiana, north of New Castle and east of the Epileptic Village, a small town called Mooreland. In 1940 the population of Mooreland was about three hundred people; in 1950 the population was three hundred, and in 1960, and 1970, and 1980, and so on. One must assume that the number three hundred, while sacred, did not represent the same persons decade after decade. A mysterious and powerful mathematical principle was at work, one by which I and my family were eventually governed. Old people died and new people were added, and thus what was shifting remained constant.

I got to be new there. I was added and shortly afterward the barber named Tony was taken away. This was in 1965. The distance between Mooreland in 1965 and a city like San Francisco in 1965 is roughly equivalent to the distance starlight must travel before we look up casually from a cornfield and see it. Sociologists and students of history imagine they know something of the United States in the sixties and seventies because they are familiar with the prevailing trends; if they drew assumptions about Mooreland based on that knowledge, they would get everything wrong. Strangely, there has never been a definitive source of information about Mooreland during a certain fifteen-year period, perhaps because there are so few people left who can reliably tell it. Many have been added since then. Many have moved on.

Not long ago my sister Melinda shocked me by saying she had always assumed that the book on Mooreland had yet to be written because no one sane would be interested in reading it. "No, no, wait," she said. "I know who might read such a book. A person lying in a hospital bed with no television and no roommate. Just lying there. Maybe waiting for a physical therapist. And then here comes a candy striper with a squeaky library cart and on that cart there is only one book—or maybe two books: yours, and *Cooking with Pork*. I can see how a person would be grateful for Mooreland then."

Everyone familiar with my childhood in Mooreland agreed with Melinda's position. One woman even said that Mooreland "is a long way to go not to be anywhere when you get there," and yet

I persisted. I felt that there was so much more to the town than its trappings. There was one main street, Broad Street, which was actually not so broad, and was the site of the town's only four-way stop sign. There were three churches: the North Christian Church and the South Christian Church, which sat at opposite ends of Broad Street like sentinels, and the Mooreland Friends Church, which was kind of in the middle of town, but tucked back on Jefferson Street at the edge of a meadow. There were no taverns, no theaters, no department stores. If a man was interested in drinking, he had to travel to Mt. Summit, to the aptly named Dog House, or to the Package Liquor Store in New Castle, about ten miles away. New Castle was, in fact, the hub of all our commercial activity, and it had everything: a fabric store, Grant's Department Store, the Castle Theater (which showed a single movie at a time, second-run, the same movie for weeks running), Becker Brothers Grocery. In Mooreland we had our own gas station and our own drugstore, where we could buy a fountain soda but no drugs. (For a while Mooreland had an actual doctor, and we could buy drugs from him, but the police eventually came and took him away.) When I was little there was a hardware store, and off and on there was a diner in what used to be somebody's house. These days it's a house again. We had a veterinarian, who could treat little animals, like cats and dogs, and big ones, like horses and cows. Mooreland was bordered at the north end by a cemetery and at the south by a funeral home. The spirit of the place, if such spirits can be said to exist, was the carnival, Poor Jack Amusements, that arrived at the end of the harvest season every August. Most people took their vacations during the week of the fair, and were there morning to night, working in a food tent or organizing one of the events, like the Horse and Pony Pull, or the Most Beautiful Baby Contest. Everyone in Mooreland believed in God (except my dad). There was no such thing as multiculturalism—no people of color, no exotic religions, no one openly homosexual (there was one old bachelor who had suspiciously good taste in furniture, but we didn't question his private life).

My parents moved to Mooreland with my brother and sister in 1955, five years after they married. (Prior to living in Mooreland they had lived in the very, very big town of Muncie; I assume those were The Dark Years.) I wasn't born until 1965, when my brother was thirteen and my sister nearly ten. My mother always cheerfully refers to me as "an afterthought," which I consider a term of immense respect and affection, in spite of Melinda's attempts to convince me otherwise.

The book that follows is about a child from Mooreland, Indiana, written by one of the three hundred. It's a memoir, and a sigh of gratitude, a way of returning. I no longer live there; I can't speak for the town or its people as they are now. Someone has taken my place. Whoever she is, her stories are her own.

BABY BOOK

The following was recorded by my mother in my baby book, under the heading MILE-STONES:

FIRST STEPS: *Nine months! Precocious!*

FIRST TEETH: *Bottom two, at eight months. Still nursing her, but she doesn't bite, thank goodness!*

FIRST SAYS "MOMMY": (blank)

FIRST SAYS "DADDY": (blank)

FIRST WAVES BYE-BYE: *As of her first birthday, she is not much interested in waving bye-bye.*

At age eighteen months, the baby book

provided a space for FURTHER MILESTONES, in which my mother wrote:

She's still very active and energetic. Her daddy calls her "Zippy," after a little chimpanzee he saw roller-skating on television. The monkey was first in one place and then zip! in another. Has twelve teeth. I'm still nursing her—she's a thin baby, and it can't hurt—but I'm thinking of weaning her to a bottle. There's no sense in trying to get her to drink from a cup. Still not talking. Dr. Heilman says she has perfectly good vocal cords, and to give it time.

On my second birthday:

Still no words from our little Zippy. She is otherwise a delight and a very sweet baby. I have turned her life over to God, to do with as He sees fit. I believe He must have a very special plan for her, because I'm sure that terrible staph infection in her ear that nearly killed her when she was a newborn must have, as the doctors feared, reached her brain. She is so quiet we hardly know she is here, and so unlike many of our friends, we can speak freely in front of her without fear she will repeat us. Little Becky Dawson walked up to Agnes Johnson in church last Sunday and called her Broad As A Barn. You know she heard that at home. We are very grateful for our little angel on her second birthday.

This entry was made on a separate piece of paper:

I've been thinking about first words, and so before I forget, here are some other important ones:

Melinda: Mama

Danny: No

Bob: Me (Mom Mary thought this was so cute; she says she first thought he was saying ma ma ma but really he was saying me me me)

My first word, of course, was Magazine.

The other day I overheard Melinda saying her night-time prayers,

6

and she was asking that someday her little sister be able to tie her shoes. Bless her heart. We all hope as much.

Under FAVORITE ACTIVITIES, Mom recorded:

God's Own Special Angel: Our Miracle Baby!

Far and away her favorite activity is rocking. She has her own rocking chair, and Bob rocks her to sleep every night. She is now refusing to take naps in her baby bed; if I try putting her down she doesn't cry or make any noise, but holds on to the rail and bounces so hard and for so long that I fear for her little spinal cord. She is not content until I put her on her rocking horse, where she bounces hard enough to cause it to hop across the floor. Eventually she grows weary and begins rocking, and then the rocking slows down, and finally she puts her head down on the hard, plastic mane and falls asleep, and I am able to move her to her bed.

Dr. Heilman is finally recognizing that all of this might be due to the fact that her umbilical cord was wrapped around her neck three times when she was born. I'm not sure why that has caused her not to grow any hair, however. She does have a few precious wisps, which I slick together with baby oil in order to put in a barrette or a ribbon.

Also she loves to go camping. Went fishing for the first time when she was only three weeks old! Her daddy is starting early! She carries a bottle with her everywhere she goes (which is everywhere). Everyone thinks I should have weaned her (she is now 30 months), but I just don't have the heart to take anything away from her.

This letter, written in my mom's tiny, precise script, was placed haphazardly in the middle of the book:

Dearest Little One: I don't know if you'll ever be able to read this, but there's a story I think you should know. When you were only five weeks old, just a tiny, tiny baby, you became very ill. You ran a terri-

bly high fever, and would not stop crying, night and day. The doctors said you had a staph infection in your ear, and that there was nothing they could do. Dr. Heilman was out of town, and we were sent to his replacement. He told us you could die at home or in the hospital. We took you home, and I didn't sleep for days. In desperation your father called our dear friends Ruth and Roland Wiser, and they drove down to Mooreland from Gary. Gary, Indiana, sweetheart, which is hours and hours away! Your father locked me in the Driftwood, our little camper, and Ruth and Roland stayed up all night, taking turns walking you so I could sleep. The next day I took you back to the doctor. He told us there was a new kind of medicine, an antibiotic, that might possibly help you, but he was not reassuring. He said there were twenty-six varieties of this medicine (the same as the alphabet); that probably only one would do you any good, and that he couldn't possibly know which one to prescribe, because they were so new. He showed me a sample case of them, little vials lined up along a spectrum, and then he just reached in and plucked one out and told me to try it. I could tell he knew it was hopeless.

We took you home and gave you the medicine. You cried yourself to sleep, and I, too, fell asleep rocking you. Just before I nodded off I told God plainly that I was letting you go, that I was delivering you into His hands. When I woke up you were silent, and I knew you were gone. I felt something damp against my arm, and when I pulled back your baby blanket, I saw that the infection had broken and run out your ear. Your skin was cool and covered with sweat, and you were sleeping deeply.

When Dr. Heilman came home he told us that the resident had been right—there was only one medicine that would have saved you, and he plucked it blindly out of the case. Dr. Heilman calls you his "Miracle

Baby" now. *Olive Overton, my dear friend from church, says that she knew you before you were born, and that it took you some time to decide whether or not you wanted to stay in this world.*

I thought you ought to know about Ruth and Roland. What they did was what it means to love someone. We are all so grateful you decided to stay.

The last entry is dated four months before my third birthday:

This weekend we went camping. After dinner little Zippy was running in circles around the campfire, drinking from her bottle, and Bob decided she'd had it long enough. He walked over to her and said, "Sweetheart, you're a big girl now, and it's time for you to give up that bottle. I want you to just give it to me, and we're going to throw it in the fire. Okay?" This was met with many protests from Danny and Melinda and me; we all felt that there was no call to take something away from one who has so little. The baby looked at us; back at her dad, and then pulled the bottle out of her mouth with an audible pop, and said, clear as daylight, "I'll make a deal with you." Her first words! Bob didn't hesitate. "What's the deal?" She said, "If you let me keep it, I'll hide it when company comes and I won't tell no-body." He thought about it for just a moment, then shook his head. "Nope. No deal." So she handed over the bottle, and we all stood together while Bob threw it in the fire. It was a little pink bottle, made of plastic. It melted into a pool.

Now that we know she can talk, all I can say is: dear God. Please give that child some hair. Amen.

H A I R

Somehow my first wig and my first really excellent pair of slippers arrived simultaneously.

Now my hair, my actual human hair which grows out of my head, was slow in coming. I was bald until I was nearly three. My head was also strangely crooked, and it happened that the little patches of wispy bird hair I did have grew only in the dents. Also my eyes were excessively large and decidedly close together. When my mother first saw me in the hospital she looked up with tears in her eyes and said to my father, "I'll love her and protect her anyway."

When my hair finally did come in, when I was three, it did so with a vengeance: thick and sprouty and curly. And not those lovely loopy curls only ungrateful men get; it was more like fourteen thousand cowlicks. In fact, left to its own devices, my head looks like a big hair alarm going off.

We tried a variety of hairstyles in those early years. The really short haircut (the Pixie, as it was then called) was my favorite, and coincidentally, the most hideous. Many large, predatory birds believed I was asking for a date. I especially liked that style because I imagined it excused me from any form of personal hygiene, which I detested. I was so opposed to bathing that I used to have a little laughing reaction every time a certain man in town walked by and said hello to me and I had to respond with "Hi, Gene."

After a year as a Pixie, my sister decided what my hair needed was "weight." Melinda executed all the haircutting ideas in our house and, in fact, cut off the tip of my earlobe one summer afternoon because she was distracted by *As the World Turns*.

The weight we added to my hair made me look like a fuzzy bush, a bush gone vague. I decided to take the scissors to it myself, and had just gotten started when my dad brought home my new wig, which he had won in a card game. I can imagine that some eight-year-olds would see an implied message in the gift of a wig; all I saw was hair, long and straight and mahogany colored, like the tail of a horse. It wasn't actually a wig—it was called a "fall," and it attached to the middle of my head by a comb, and then fell down my back.

Now because it was a fall and not a wig, there was a problem with all that front part, like the bang part, and those side areas that swooped up into little points, but I decided to take what I could get. I had never before shown any interest in my physical self—my sister swore I had no pride—so when I asked her for bobby pins to help hold my new hair on, she gave them to me without so much as a snicker.

I was admiring myself in the bathroom mirror when Melinda came in and asked me, a bit sheepishly, if I wanted her old house slippers. She had outgrown them, and had never really liked them anyway. I turned and looked at her suspiciously, thinking this was surely a trap, but she was genuine.

I wore my new hair into her bedroom. Her room was painted the color of the best sky, and next to her bed she had a wicker chair and on the chair was a homemade, stuffed clown. It was a very benevolent-looking thing, but once when she was away at a friend's house I snuck into her bed and it began talking to me in the dark, so I kept a wide berth.

Without ceremony, she gave me the slippers. They were made of the most fabulous, long, fake fur, and when worn, made the human foot look like a pink, oval biscuit. The fur kind of sprouted up off the top of the slippers and hung down to the floor. They made a delicious little snicking sound as I walked, too. I remember no house slippers before or after this pair.

Yes, I had beautiful long hair, and yes, I had beautiful slippers, but I was still myself, and there was only one thing I could think to do to keep from bursting. I decided to go play rodeo on my bicycle with the purple banana seat and the sissy bars. It was my stallion, and we had been down a dusty road or two. As I climbed on and started speeding down the street, I could feel my sister's newfound respect fading like an old star, but I couldn't stop. I turned the corner of Charles and Jefferson as if nothing could touch me—I rode faster and faster. As I rode past the Kizers' house, where all the mangy foster children lived, one of them shouted, "Nice wig!" And I yelled back, my face bent close to the handle-bars, "It's my real hair!" And then another block up, Ruth Kennedy shouted did I know I was wearing my slippers, and I yelled, "They're my actual feet!" And it was a long time before I went back home.

THE LION

My dad asked me what I wanted to be when I grew up and I said I'd have to think about it. I questioned some friends, and discovered that these were the options available to me: ice skater, cowboy, teacher of little kids, large animal veterinarian. I didn't really, in my deepest heart, want to be any of those. I began to fear that I might live my whole life without gainful employment, as most of the rest of my family had.

Dad told me to think about what I enjoyed doing most, and how I wanted people to see me when I was grown, and I set my mind to that. I was deeply, tragically in love with Telly Savalas at the time, and carried his picture around in an old wallet my grandma, Mom Mary, had given me. My love for him made me dissatisfied with my own life.

I was in a state all during that career time, and then one night, just before I fell asleep, I realized what I wanted to be. The next morning I jumped down the stairs, skipping every other one, so that my mom called me Herd of Elephants. I went outside, where my dad was puttering in his tool shed, and told him I wanted to belong to the Mafia. He asked what did I mean when I said that, and I said like in the movies, and he nodded.

A few days later he came home with a framed certificate printed on very genuine yellow paper that said I was an official, lifetime member of the Mafia. Some of it was in Italian and some of it was just in an Italian accent. A man named Leonardo "The Lion" Gravitano Salvatore had signed it with a tall, threatening signature.

After that my life changed, and I mean for the better. Hardly anyone ever bothered me, except for my sister, who must have belonged to whatever is bigger and meaner than the Mafia. Maybe the Jehovah's Witnesses. She dared even to lock me out of the house one night when my parents were away, when there was a bat on the front porch that was clearly diseased and looking for hair. My brother came from out of nowhere and unlocked the door, and just in time, too. Back in the house I gave my sister a whole host of menacing, Italian faces, which she pretended to ignore.

DAD ASKED ME did I want to learn to dance and I said yes. He put the "Theme from a Summer Place" on the record player and then had me stand on top of his feet while he led me in a box step. Mom said we were quite a couple of dancers. It was so nice whirling around the living room to that summery music that for a moment I forgot about Telly Savalas and my own life of crime and was just carried away. Then the song ended and my dad stepped back and gave me a little bow and asked who loves ya, baby, and I laughed out loud and said *you do*.

QUALITIES OF LIGHT,
OR DISASTERS
INVOLVING ANIMALS

For one whole year I sighed every time I was asked to do anything. I felt incredibly put upon. My parents were patient with it for a few months, and then both began saying, in a rather clipped and hysterical way, *don't sigh*, immediately after making some small request.

For instance, my dad might ask, "Have

you done your feeding?" Which meant had I fed the few animals I had begged for and bet my life against, and I would stop what I was doing, which was probably sitting absolutely still watching *Gilligan's Island,* and sigh. And he would speedy-quick say *don't sigh,* but I was way ahead of him and already done sighing. Sometimes I would rouse myself and go feed the starving animals, but sometimes I would continue just very actively sitting there until he became agitated and got up to do it himself, meaning to shame me, which didn't work.

My parents went from reprimanding to giving very thunderous looks, which also didn't stop me, until finally on one occasion, with the dogs howling for mercy outside, my father snapped. I was standing in the doorway between the living room and the den, and he covered the distance between us so quickly he appeared to levitate. He took me by the shoulders and backed me all the way down the length of the long living room, his face in mine, staring at me like a deranged cow, saying over and over, *don't sigh,* through his clenched teeth. So I stopped sighing.

MY EARLIEST MEMORY is of a wolf in my baby bed. I have made that claim for as long as I can remember, and for years my family treated it as just more evidence of whatever. My mother finally solved the mystery of how a memory can be so hallucinatory and yet be true.

When I was born we had two dogs: the great, noble, and legendary German shepherd, Kai; and Tiger, who was some sort of beagle-shaped zeppelin with unusual bowel function and tragically short legs. My sister picked Tiger out from the Diseased and Deformed Puppy Room at the animal shelter.

Kai's lineage was embarrassingly good. Either my father won him gambling, or else my parents sold a fourth sibling to buy him, because he was magnificent, and had no rival in Mooreland. His father was black and silver and his mother was snow white, and Kai turned out to be the color of coins falling from a winter sky.

He was mature by the time I was born, and had developed a number of patterns in his work as our guardian. He despised insurance salesmen, trick-or-treaters, and rats in equal measure. When I was learning to walk my mother used to take me out into the yard while she hung up laundry, and Kai paced the sidewalk between me and the street. If I got too close to the edge of the yard, he would simply pick me up by the seat of my pants and move me back into the grass.

He didn't allow fighting or tickling among family members, but took great pleasure in watching my mom and sister and me color in our coloring books, and could eat an enormous amount of popcorn, one piece at a time, which he caught in the air.

His most serious and important work was at night. As soon as Dad turned out the lights, Kai walked upstairs and looked at my brother in his bed, at my sister in hers, then clip, clip, clip down the stairs where he checked on both of my parents. Finally, he would walk over to my baby bed, and putting both paws on the railing, lean his massive head down and look at me. Assured we were all present and accounted for, he lay down at the foot of my parents' bed, let out a sigh, and slept.

And one night, when the light was just so, my new mind lit up, and I decided it was time to begin remembering, and out of all the faces I loved so much, I started with Kai's.

He died when I was six, of heartworms. They are a terrible danger in Indiana.

MY BEST FRIEND was Julie Newman, a little red-haired girl. Her parents, Big Dave and Debbie, owned the gas station next to our house, and also the car wash (which sometimes worked and was sometimes frozen), farther down Charles Street, and a row of three apartments behind the hardware store. It was a little empire. But their greatest piece of real estate by far was their 120-acre farm, which sat three miles or so outside Mooreland. Of all the places in the wide world, Julie's farm was my favorite place, and I learned some very shocking things about life there.

For instance, when pigs were born, the runt of the litter was almost always just straightaway thrown on the dead baby pig pile, since it was bound to die anyway. This was a practice I had protested so often and so loudly that one day Big Dave allowed Julie and me to take a runt into the house to try to raise it.

There is hardly a thing in this world as perfectly cute as a baby pig, and even Julie, who was all business in the farrowing house, couldn't help but rub its little snoot and admire its dark pink color.

"Let me hold him now. Hey, Julie. You've been holding him for a long time. Let me hold him now. Hey."

We decided to name him Sam. We had many plans for him. We were going to enter him in the Mooreland Fair Parade on Kiddie Day in the Pets category, with maybe a ruffle around his neck. We were going to teach him to give us rides on his back. We were going to build him an apartment house out of cardboard boxes and keep him with us forever, all the way up till the time Julie and I bought our own farm, where he would be installed as the Main Pig.

As we got close to the Newmans' house, the German shepherd who lived in the pen went wild. His name was Biz, and he was kept only to guard their gas station at night. No one but Big Dave had ever touched him. He was deeply and truly Satan's own, and yet Julie, with her strange diplomacy, always defended him. If I said, for instance, "Isn't Biz the most evil creature ever?" she would answer, "Naaaahhh," in that long, eloquent way that was the Newman verbal hallmark.

Biz threw himself hideously at the fence, snarling and snorting through his big ugly nose.

"Ugh. I hate that dog," I said, bending my body around the little pig.

"Nowww," Julie answered, her big chastisement.

Debbie was in the kitchen frying dinner. Dinner at the Newmans' always, always involved the Fry Daddy. I don't think they ever actually turned it off. The food groups as represented by Debbie were: Fried, Meat, Bread, Coke, and Ice Cream. She was an excellent cook.

Debbie was a big fat saucy woman. Some women carry their weight at the top of their bodies, and some at the bottom, but Debbie was perfectly round. One time we were all gathered out in the pig lot trying to catch a stray sow. The sow was notoriously ill tempered and quite large. Big Dave was there, and Julie's older brother, David Lee, and two or three farmhands and Julie, Debbie, and me. We had formed a circle around the errant sow, and each of us was holding something we could swing, if necessary. We three women each had a barn board plank that we held in front of us like a loose picket fence. I was all in favor of the sow being caught by one of the men, yet another confession of my failure as a farmhand, but Debbie was whooping and hollering for all she was worth. She couldn't have been more than five feet tall, but there she stood yelling, "SouEEE! PigEEE! Come on, souEEE! PigEEE!"

No one else was calling with such gusto, and as Debbie got more heated up, a generalized jocularity began to spread among us, which in this case took the form of a long snicker and some foot shuffling.

The sow was as far from Debbie as she could be and highly agitated, running first toward Dave and then toward Larry, but as we got more quiet and Debbie got louder, the sow slowed down and turned and looked Debbie's way. Eventually the pig stopped moving altogether and just stood looking at Debbie, who was still souEEEing to beat the band. Just as Dave was about to slip a rope around the sow's neck, she bent over and started running straight for Debbie. I'm talking about a missile-shaped, one thousand pounds of hard meat. With teeth.

There was a moment of silence while all of us waited for the dreaded convergence of the twain. The pig was running flat-out, dead on. Debbie bent her fat little knees and held out her plank. She never blinked.

The pig hit her in such a way that Debbie went flying straight up in the air, belly first, truly like a human weather balloon. She hovered for a second, and then came down, completely stiff, still clutching her barn board out in front of her. She landed in the mud with such force that it nearly buried her.

I have never heard grown men laugh that hard. One by one they dropped to their knees, peeling off their seed caps and wiping their eyes of tears. All the while Debbie lay spread-eagled and stuck like an artifact, yelling, "You goddamned worthless idiots! Get over here and help! And where'd the goddamned pig go?!"

The sow, completely forgotten, stood placid and perplexed in the middle of the barn lot, next to the old Marathon Jeep the chickens used to roost in. David Lee just walked over and roped her, all the while holding his side and repeating, "Oh, Lord. Whoo. Oh, man. Whooeee."

WE CARRIED LITTLE SAM in through the mud room, which was the size of most living rooms. It held two deep freezers and four or five saddles on saw horses, fourteen tons of strange farm implements, beautiful leather tack, and mud. On the wall was an old, poster-size photograph of Geronimo.

We stole a clean towel in the laundry room, and had just laid Sam down on top of the heating grate when Debbie came in out of the kitchen.

"What do you think you're doing, bringing that pig into my house?" Her head was cocked to the side, and she had her fists balled up where her hips would have been.

"We're gonna save it from the dead baby pig pile, Debbie, and enter it in the Fair Parade, and take it to the farm we buy when we're older."

"That pig better *not* shit on my clean towel, do you hear me, Julie Ann?"

I looked up at Debbie with my most sincere Have A Heart face, but Julie just kept rubbing the piglet's side. Finally she said, quietly, "Nowwww, Mom." Debbie harummphed, and went back to the kitchen.

Julie and I sat by the pig until late into the night, feeding it water from an eye dropper and keeping it warm. I told Julie many times how impressed I was by her compassion, which was not always in evidence, and how good and right I thought it was to try to save the Poor and Unfortunate Sam.

"Mmm hmmm," she said, with just the slightest upturn on the last syllable to let me know she agreed with me.

Toward morning, exhausted by our lifesaving efforts, we fell into bed. We woke at the same time, and sprang up to check on our little charge. He was just as we had left him, but when Julie pulled back the receiving blanket it became clear, alas, that he was not breathing.

I sat down hard with disappointment. "Oh, no," I said, tearfully, rubbing his little pink belly.

Julie said nothing, just picked him up and headed for the mud room door. I was grabbing my hat in preparation for the funeral when I saw her step outside and sling Sam by the back leg into Biz's pen.

I froze, aghast, my hat dangling from my hand.

"Julie Ann Newman!" I said, nearly whispering with indignation.

Julie stopped me with her hand on my arm. I have never in my life seen kinder or more sparkly eyes than hers, and every time she gave me the silencing look I realized how much she knew that I would never know. The arc of that piglet through the air into the dog pen contained more comedy than I will ever see again in my life, but my heart still ached. She didn't laugh, and I didn't cry.

WHEN IT BECAME completely impossible for me to live without a pet chicken, my dad took me out to Tinker Jones's, where there was fowl of every variety. Going to Tink's was good and bad: there were chicks and truly excellent things, and there was also our Driftwood trailer.

The Driftwood was a little teardrop-shaped camper my parents had for many years. It was perfectly compact and nicely appointed; it slept six comfortably. In all the camping pictures, before and after I was born, the Driftwood is sitting there sweetly. My mom made little curtains for it, and my dad, in his relentless quest for organization, had it packed in such a way that we could have survived a nuclear winter without going hungry or running out of propane. My parents sold it for god knows what reason, and they sold it to Tinker Jones, who parked it in a turnaround in his driveway and never moved it again. It sat there for years and years, and eventually a tree fell on it and Tink never moved the tree, either, so it came to resemble a piece of found sculpture. Going to the Jones's was like visiting one's children in a loveless and ill-run orphanage.

I figure heaven will be a scratch-and-sniff sort of place, and one of my first requests will be the Driftwood in its prime, while it was filled with our life. And later I will ask for the smell of my dad's truck, which was a combination of basic truck (nearly universal), plus his cologne (Old Spice), unfiltered Lucky Strikes, and when I was very lucky, leaded gasoline. If I could have gotten my nose close enough I would have inhaled leaded gasoline until I was retarded. The tendency seemed to run in my family; as a boy my uncle Crandall had an ongoing relationship with a gas can he kept in the barn. Later he married and divorced the same woman four times, sometimes marrying other women in between, including one whose name was, honestly, Squirrelly.

Later still I will ask for the smell of Tinker Jones's backyard. He had a small pond, on which floated white ducks and mallards and geese, and a big barn where the chickens roosted. There were guinea hens and shy quail hiding in the bushes at the edge of the woods. The air was permeated with the smell of the birds. It was lovely.

I made a deal with my dad—we were big on deals. I had promised that if he would let me have my own chicken I would take care of her promptly every day, and spend time with her, and never sigh when he reminded me to claim her eggs. In return he would build her a nice big cage, which he did, and a roosting box filled with fresh straw. My other part of the bargain, the tricky part, was that I had exactly the distance between Tinker's house and our house, about eleven miles, to tame her.

I could choose from any of the young chickens in the barn, but it wasn't hard. I wasn't swept away by the cute chicks, and I didn't covet any of the elaborately colored or fluffy-legged ones. The minute I saw my chicken I knew.

She was a young banty hen, a junior-sized chicken, and her feathers were black-and-white speckled. I named her Speckles. Tink put her in a box for me, and she and I climbed into the back of Dad's truck, which had a camper shell on it at the time, and we headed for home.

I opened her box with no chicken-taming technique at my disposal, just my utter good will. I don't remember what actually transpired between us, but by the time we got home and Dad opened the tailgate, Speckles was sitting on my shoulder, and if I made kissing sounds at her she turned and pecked me lightly on the lips.

I have noticed that otherwise sensitive and intelligent people will go to great lengths to decry the love between a person and a chicken, claiming that, of all things, chickens are not *smart enough* to love. Well, I'm here to tell you: I've seen women passionately devoted to men who couldn't pile bricks, and whole families of slack-jawed nose pickers held together by "love," not to mention all those people who curl up at night with dogs that have gunk running out of their eyes, dogs who earlier peed where they were about to walk and spent ten minutes licking their own wormy butts.

Speckles and I loved each other. Dad never had to tell me to feed her—I couldn't wait to see her every day. In the mornings she hopped out of her box when she heard me coming, and did something like a tail-feather wag as I opened the pen door. When I sat down she hopped onto my lap, and then let me lift her up onto my shoulder, where she would sometimes just stand very officiously. Other times she sat down, tucking her legs up underneath her and making little happy chicken sounds, the bird equivalent of a purring cat.

And there it was every day, a perfect little egg, left like an offering. Fortunately I didn't acquire Speckles as a food source, because when a banty egg is broken open in a frying pan, the whole affair is about the size of a silver dollar.

I was so fond of Speckles that Dad decided we should get a rooster and raise some babies. He went alone to pick the rooster out, and chose the most brazenly attractive of the banty males. He was blue and excessively strutty. As far as I know, there are only two names for roosters in the history of the world, Red and Chanticleer, and we could hardly call him Red.

So Chanticleer came to live with us, and life changed radically. I cannot in good taste report the relationship between Speckles and Chanty, except to say that he was relentless and she spent a great deal of time running from him. He must have been accustomed to servicing five or six hens at Tink's, because he never stopped. I liked him not at all.

After Chanticleer came to stay with us I could no longer get in Speckles' pen with her. Like any abusive male, her husband first separated her from her family and friends. I had to just stand on the outside with my fingers hooked in the wire, looking at her longingly. I think Speckles would have looked at me with yearning as well, except she was generally wild-eyed, and had to keep glancing over her shoulder.

One day at school I decided to just tell my dad how I felt about Chanticleer, how I wanted him to go back to the farm even though he was so extra good-looking. I thought about it all the way home. My resolve got me safely past scary old Edythe's yard, where normally I would have become all skittery, afraid she would walk out of her terrifying house and wag her chin whiskers at me. I decided to just go straight to Speckles and explain the whole thing to her.

Dad had built the cage behind our house, where it would be in the shade almost all day, and as I marched past Dad's tilty tool shed all I noticed was the quiet. When I got to the cage I saw why: one whole side of the cage was ripped apart, and inside there was nothing but feathers.

I stood frozen for just a moment, the way children do, my synapses firing and misfiring like crazy, trying to make sense of the senseless, and then I turned and ran into the house, dropping my books and my Honorary Mouseketeer corduroy jacket along the way, and threw myself onto the couch. I wailed and sobbed with such abandon that my mother must have feared some real calamity, and when I told her what had happened she just sat on the edge of the couch beside me, rubbing my back and telling me how sorry she was.

Then my sister came in.

"What's wrong with her?" she asked, pointing to my hiccuping body.

"Her chicken got killed." My mom tried, I honestly believe, to say it with real sympathy, but she had not truly known Chicken Love, and there was just the slightest warble in her voice, if I may risk such a description. It was enough to send my sister over the edge.

She tried to say, "oh, dear," but it came out as just a big snort, and soon her legs had collapsed and she was laughing so hard she was making no sound and wiping tears off her face.

My sister's general gaiety was interrupted by my dad coming home from work, or wherever he went during the day. When I tried to tell him about Speckles I cried even harder. I was completely undone.

It is difficult for parents to face such grief in their children, and Dad's temper was not mild to begin with. He turned rather scarlet and puffed up like a blowfish. Announcing that he knew exactly which dogs had done it (he had seen them loose in our yard before and had warned their owner once), he took down his police-issue .357 Magnum, a gun large enough to kill, say, a mastodon, and went flying out the door.

He came back an hour later and said the dogs had been taken care of, whatever that meant. I was too stunned to ask and didn't really want to know. Then he went out and dismantled the ravaged cage and cleaned up the feathers. Except for the bare spot, he left nothing that might remind me of what had been there.

Later that evening he took a single little egg out of his breast pocket, which he had found under the roosting box. I put it in the refrigerator, on a nest made out of a blue handkerchief. Over the next few days and weeks I took it out and looked at it many times, but I didn't know what to do with it. I kept it so long that whatever was inside it completely dried up, and finally it was so light and in-substantial in my hand that it seemed barely to exist. It was just a sigh of a thing.

JULIE HIT ME
THREE TIMES

The teachers all thought that Julie couldn't talk. I knew she could, but she didn't want to, because she sounded funny. Her brother, David Lee, who was basically a heathen, knocked all her front baby teeth out when she was only two years old, so she never learned to talk exactly right. Maybe there was one little snaggletooth left on the side, I can't remember, but if any teeth survived they got knocked out later the same summer when she was on a trail ride in Brown County and her horse leaned over too far to take a drink out of a creek. Julie slid right down the horse's neck and face first into the water. There's a picture of her in the family album. She's wearing a little yellow shirt, and she's pulling down the neck of it to reveal a bloody scrape that runs from her chin to her collarbone. She's looking up at the camera, but she has her head turned a little to the side, and she is nothing but proud.

I myself had been a late talker, and had saved up a fair amount of words as a result, so I did all of my own talking plus all of Julie's. I knew what she meant to say without her even looking at me. For instance, on the first day of kindergarten our stupid teacher Mrs. Dockerty tried to give Julie a blue crayon for coloring and Julie just sat staring at her desk and wouldn't take it. I didn't pipe up right away, I let Mrs. Dockerty get good and frustrated, and then I said from my desk right next to Julie's that Julie couldn't abide a blue crayon and somebody better give her green. Mrs. Dockerty took offense.

"I believe Julie can speak for herself," she said with her prim little voice out of her prim little nose.

"Well, good luck" was all I said, and I looked back down and started coloring with my red crayon, which was perfectly okay with me.

And after a little while Mrs. Dockerty slipped Julie a green crayon on the sly, without even looking at me, because she couldn't bear to think that I had been right, and Julie just went to town on her sailboat. She colored that whole page green.

From then on I did all of Julie's talking in kindergarten, although Mrs. Dockerty pretended she couldn't hear me, like Julie was actually speaking for herself. That went okay until one day at quiet time when Julie and I were lying next to each other on our rugs, and I saw a particular look pass over her face.

"Mrs. Dockerty, Julie's got to poop."

All the kids who were awake started rolling around on their rugs and snickering.

Mrs. Dockerty pointed at me with her prim little finger. "You lie down and mind your own business," she hissed through her small teeth.

"I'm just trying to help. You don't want her to poop in her drawers, do ya?," which made one boy, Jackie, who was bad, roll right off his rug and into the Lincoln Logs. Everybody was laughing, in fact, except for Julie, who really did have to poop, and was starting to look worried.

"Wha—where do you hear such things? Don't answer me. Julie, go to the bathroom if you need to."

So Julie got up and went to the bathroom, and even though she had done nothing wrong she fell in Mrs. Dockerty's estimation, and for the rest of the year Mrs. Dockerty didn't like either one of us. On my end-of-the-year report card all she wrote was "Is disruptive in class. Colors outside the lines. Talks out of turn." When I showed it to my parents, they read it out loud to me, and my mom said, "Good for you, sweetheart." And my dad gave me a little pat on the back.

I TOOK TO TALKING for Julie the way some children take to water. I talked for her at school and at home, and her parents were nothing but grateful, because they were completely worn out from trying to read her mind.

One night when we were in the second grade, when I was at home with my actual parents, Debbie called to ask me if Julie wanted to spend some of the money in her savings account (which was hefty—she never spent a dime) on a new saddle they had seen.

"I don't know," I answered. "Put her on the phone."

Debbie handed the phone to Julie. There was a long silence, then Julie gave the phone back to her mom.

"No, she would prefer not to."

"I told her fool father that she'd use her old saddle till it was dust before she'd crack open her piggy bank, but he wouldn't listen."

"I'd like a new saddle," I said wistfully, meaning I'd like a new saddle and a new horse to put it on, and the Newmans' many, many gorgeous acres and their excellent farmhouse with a bumper pool table in the dining room.

"Jarvis, you need a saddle like a hole in the head. I'm scared every time you get on a horse. You're an accident waiting to happen."

"Debbie!" I did my best to sound wounded. "I'm very careful when I ride."

"*Julie's* very careful when you ride. You'd break your scrawny neck if it wasn't for her. Now go to bed. You've got school tomorrow." And she hung up. Debbie talked more than anybody in that whole family.

WE WERE ON our way home from a basketball game. It was snowing enough that Big Dave was carefully negotiating every turn and every stop. We were listening to another game on the AM radio, between two teams who could potentially play Blue River in the sectionals. Dave was crazy for basketball. He had been the all-time leading scorer in Mooreland, back when my elementary school had also been a high school. (In the 1960s the county schools were consolidated and the high school was moved to a new building four miles down the highway.) Dave had been so important to the team, in fact, that when he got Debbie pregnant early in their senior year, she refused to marry him so he could finish out the season, with the result that at their wedding she was so pregnant she had to rest her little bouquet on her enormous belly. That baby was Connie, Julie and David Lee's older sister, who was no longer with us. She had been Called Home in the sixth grade, under very tragic circumstances we all preferred not to discuss.

Julie and I were in the back seat of the Newmans' big gray car, which always smelled like the barn, but in a pleasant way. I was talking to Julie and also answering for her. The conversation was going quite well, and then Debbie turned around in her seat and said in a fast and kind of hard way, "You talk too much." Which would have been humiliating enough all by itself, but I made it worse by not answering at all, by just shutting up in the most desperate and silent way I possibly could, and the absence of my voice in the car was so noticeable that everybody started to laugh. I made it all the rest of the way home without crying and without talking, and by the time we pulled into Newmans' barn lot the car was pretty doggone quiet, and Julie was looking at me like she maybe had a few things she'd like to say, but I'd have been hanged before I would have said them for her.

JULIE'S GRANNY AND GRANDDAD were named Genevieve and Kim. Big Dave looked like exactly half of each of them, and Julie looked like exactly half of each of her parents, except for some things that had passed down undiluted from Kim to Big Dave to Julie. They all had the same red hair, and kind of reddish-tan skin, and hard, square faces with sharp cheekbones. And you couldn't get a word out of any of them. Kim was just a big, old, hardworking farmer. He smoked cigars and drank moonshine, and every New Year's Eve we got to spend the night at his house and shoot off shotguns at midnight and drink some moonshine out of Dixie cups. It was pure poison.

He got sick when we were in the third grade, but Julie never told me. Word never got to me at all, until my mom told me one day after school that Kim had been taken to the hospital, and he died that night. Julie was at school the next day as if nothing had happened, but it had so much happened that I was obliged to say something. We were out on the playground, on the sidewalk next to the school, and I stopped Julie and tried to look her in the eye.

"I heard about your granddad, Julie, and I'm really sorry."

She looked at me, and I was completely undone when I saw that tears were standing in her eyes. I had never, ever seen her cry. Then she pulled back her fist and punched me so hard in the belly that my diaphragm collapsed like an old balloon. I let out a big whoosh, doubled over, and then toppled over onto my butt. I was staring right at my dirty old black-and-white saddle oxfords with liver-colored soles, and making a big groaning sound trying to re-fill my lungs. She let me catch my breath and then offered me her hand. She helped me up and we went straight on to play two-square, which was where we were heading in the first place, and she beat me every single game, as she always did. Julie could have beaten the people who invented two-square.

I went to Granddad Kim's funeral, nervously. Inside the mortuary Dave and his brothers and their wives were gathered around the casket. Julie was sitting miserably on a white padded chair up against the wall. Her parents had stuck her in a pretty, green dress, which I was certain was making her entirely more unhappy than the fact of the wake. Julie in a dress was like the rest of us in quicksand. I avoided her eye, and I never spoke to her, but I knew she'd never forget I had been there. Julie never forgot anything.

SHE WOULD HAVE PREFERRED to be completely invisible, but God had other plans for Julie. Her hair, which was the strangest color, hung down her back like a slick red curtain. And her large round eyes and her eyebrows were all the same warm color as her hair, and it didn't really matter what she did or how she felt about it, she was stuck with being beautiful.

Watching her work on the tractor engine one afternoon I became hypnotized by the way panels of her hair kept falling forward and framing her face. It was obviously nothing but annoying to her, but I just wanted to reach out and touch it. I wanted to reach out and touch it and reach out and touch it, so I reached out and touched it, and she quick stood up and punched me in the arm. She had a way of punching with the knuckle of her middle finger raised slightly which, magically, completely separated the muscle from the bone.

"Ow! Why'd you hit me?!" I yelled, rubbing my arm.

"Why'd you touch my hair?!" she yelled back.

"Because you're so beautiful!" I shouted, which caused her to punch me in the other arm, even harder.

I jumped down off the tractor and started to head for the house. Julie went back to the greasy tractor engine, as if nothing had happened. I didn't have full use of my arms, because they were both kind of tingly and numb, and so I couldn't fully defend myself from Red, the Newmans' wretched, oversized rooster. As I stepped out of the pole barn he charged me. I squealed and went left. He charged again. By employing a sophisticated pattern of squeals and zigzags I made it halfway across the barn lot before he came at me seriously. By this time Sarge, the Newmans' extra nice three-legged dog was barking, and Biz, the Newmans' most viciously evil dog was hurling himself at his pen, and all I could do was stand there wailing with my arms hanging uselessly at my sides. I had to keep looking down to make sure I hadn't lost my fingers.

Red was about a foot from me when Julie came flying out of the barn with a stick, which she threw at Red as if it were a frisbee, hitting him in the side of the head and causing him to do a very comical rooster roll across the dusty barn lot. When he stood up he actually shook his head a few times, trying to clear it. Then she leaned down and scratched Sarge behind the ear a few times, which made him wiggle his hind parts so hard his leg stump thumped on the ground. Then she quick picked up the basketball lying next to the chicken coop and shot an eighteen-foot jump shot at the hoop on the side of the pole barn, sunk it, ran on back into the barn, and fixed the tractor.

I thanked her for rescuing me by bringing her her favorite lunch: MoonPie and a Pepsi, and she wasn't mad at me at all. But the next day I had two Julie-shaped bruises, one on each arm, in addition to a small sister-shaped bruise I'd gotten in church the previous Sunday, on the underside of my arm. I was very proud of them and didn't want to wear a shirt even though it was only forty degrees, because I thought I looked like Lydia the Tattooed Lady.

DANIEL

He was a firstborn son; healthy and beautiful and given a strong Biblical name, to see him through, I reckoned, his time with lions, whatever they were. He wore a coonskin cap like Davy Crockett and rode his tricycle for miles around the block. In a picture of him at two he's looking at the photographer rather than the camera. His blond hair waves over his forehead. His lips are so full they look puffy, and his big brown eyes are so beseeching, they beg so much mercy, that you're tempted to look away. Tears are streaming down his face.

It's a wrenching photograph in one way, but also pleasing, because from one angle he's just another gorgeous little boy crying about having his picture taken.

MY MOM AND I were sitting on the couch early in the morning, winter dark. I was curled up against her as she worked on a sweater. Dan and Melinda were getting ready for school; I didn't go to school yet and had begun to believe that kindergarten wasn't in my best interests anyway. When my siblings left in the morning I stood with my nose pressed against the screen door long enough to imprint a little waffle pattern of rust that I would try not to disturb for the rest of the day.

My brother was a senior in high school and still rode the school bus every morning to the new high school down the highway. I gathered from conversations I overheard that this was some grave form of injustice, especially in light of the fact that my sister, who was only a sophomore, rode to school in a car with a friend, which meant Danny had to leave earlier than Melinda. In addition to having an unfair ride, most days Melinda got into the bathroom first and then wouldn't come out, even while Danny stood outside the door nervously, watching the clock tick toward the time he had to go.

The kitchen and the den, in which we did all our living, were actually one long room divided by a "breakfast bar" my dad had built, and at the end of this room was our only bathroom. Danny knocked on the bathroom door, which was wooden, painted vaguely green, and had a tarnished brass doorknob that sometimes turned too far to the right. I had been convinced sixty-four times that I was stuck in the bathroom forever, my only hope of escape being to climb through the window, which was painted shut and led directly out onto the silver fuel-oil tank. Eventually I would remember to turn the knob back to the left and would escape just before I was forced to bellow for the volunteer fire department.

Inside the door was a little hook-and-loop that served as a lock. My parents never locked the bathroom door, but Melinda and I did even if we were only going in to brush our teeth or look for a towel. I personally believed that the bathroom door should be kept shut at all times, ever since my hamster Skippy had escaped from his little cage and mysteriously drowned in my potty chair. My sister could do a dreadfully accurate imitation of the look on Skippy's face when we found him, and she preferred to perform it at odd times, just so I would never forget that I was implicated in the death of an innocent rodent.

Dan knocked on the bathroom door with long and serious pauses in between the knocks. Melinda shouted, "I'll be out in a minute!" in way that suggested she had no such intentions.

"Lindy! Let your brother in the bathroom; he has to leave soon," Mom said, without dropping a stitch.

Melinda didn't answer. Dan looked at his watch, which was attached to a two-inch wide, brown leather band, then raised his fist and knocked again, harder this time.

"I'll be out soon!" Melinda shouted, with a sort of barely concealed glee.

"Lindy! Your brother needs to get in the bathroom!"

Danny sat down. He stood up. He paced, then knocked on the door, then sat down. I was thinking this would be an excellent time to have my little blue tape recorder out, but I didn't dare get up to find it. There was something about the way Dan stood up for the last time that made me instinctively turn and look at my mom, who stopped knitting. A mighty sound, a sort of giving way, came from the direction of the bathroom, and by the time I looked over, the vaguely green bathroom door was off the hinges and lying on the couch beside me, the little eye still dangling from the little hook lock.

Melinda was just sitting on the edge of the tub, completely dressed, her hair combed, her makeup on. Danny took one look at her, then raised his left arm and slapped her open-handed hard enough that she fell in the tub. Her wail was instantaneous, but my mom and I continued to sit as silent as stumps, watching the scene unfold. Danny turned to the sink, where he quickly brushed his teeth and ran a comb through his hair. He was out of the bathroom before Melinda was out of the tub. Mom and I watched him shrug into his winter coat and walk out into the dark to wait on the corner for the bus.

"What are you going to <u>do</u> about this?!" Melinda cried, her hand against her cheek, which was already swelling, and red.

"Well, Melinda. For heaven's sake, you provoked him mercilessly."

"You love him better than me! He's your favorite!" Melinda said, as she grabbed her coat and made an angry exit.

Mom and I looked at each other. "I'd have slapped her, too," she said. "I would have had to ask someone else to rip the door off the hinges, but *then* I would have slapped her."

AT SCHOOL MELINDA was something of a hero. All of her friends gathered around her to hear the story, then spent the day giving Danny thunderous looks. Even some of his own friends were surprised, but he refused to say anything in his own defense.

By the time Dan and Melinda got home from school, I had studied that bathroom door long and hard. I kept imagining the moment my dad came home from work and saw it lying there on the couch, as strange as a tooth disconnected from a head. My impulse was to take both of Danny's hands in mine and say, "Goodbye, brother."

Melinda had been thinking the same thing. As we all sat in the den waiting for Dad's truck to hit the two big holes filled with icy, muddy water in front of the house, she kept saying to Dan, "Any minute now! Hmmmm. I wonder what Dad's going to say about this one. You pulled off the bathroom door and slapped your sister in the face. What time do you have there, Daniel?"

Dan sat stone silent, staring at the wall, flexing his jaw muscles, which were already more developed than other men's biceps.

Mooreland was so quiet we could hear Dad's truck at the four-way stop at the corner. We heard him turn onto Charles Street; the dreaded splashing into the puddles; the pause while he put the truck in park, then gathered up his wallet, his lighter, his gun. The closing of the truck door, muffled in the cold. And then he was in the house and putting his things down on the dining room table. He parted the heavy curtains that separated the den from the living room.

No one said a word. He glanced at our faces and then saw the door on the couch.

"Somebody want to tell me what happened here?" Dad's voice was so deep we felt it before we heard it.

"Well, Bob," Mom began. "Melinda was in the bathroom getting ready for school and Dan needed to get in there, and she . . . procrastinated a bit, and Dan, well, forcibly removed the door and found Melinda sitting on the edge of the tub, so he slapped her, then got ready for school and left."

Dad nodded. "He knocked a few times, did he?"

"Yes, that's right. He knocked a few times."

"Then he just tore the door off, found Lindy sitting on the tub, completely ready? So he slapped her? Did he hurt her?"

Mom looked at Melinda, who appeared to have been injured in a variety of ways, none of them precisely physical. Melinda nodded vigorously, and started to say, "I fell into the tub!" but Mom interrupted her. "No, he didn't really hurt her."

Dad had yet to move from the position he was in when he first saw the detached door. He bit his bottom lip a moment and studied Dan, who wouldn't meet his eye.

"Son? You think you could help me put this door back up?"

And so they set about it. Melinda stormed out of the den and stomped upstairs to her bedroom, which was so cold, I knew, she could see her breath. My mom fetched my coloring book and I sat on the couch pretending I was deeply engaged in making Maleficent look so scary she could actually put a lovely, innocent princess to sleep for a hundred years. In fact I was keeping one eye firmly on my dad and brother, who were working together without any visible tension. It seemed to me that Dan should have shown some sign that he had won, but he didn't. Whatever battle he was fighting was so complicated it couldn't be described in terms as simple as victory, or loss.

THERE SHE IS

No event was more important than the Mooreland Fair, and no one was more honored than the Queen, so the year my sister ran for Fair Queen, 1972, I broke open my piggy bank to put all my money in the decorated coffee can that sat in front of her picture in the Big Tent at the entrance to the fair. The queen was decided by a process called "a-penny-a-vote," which was modeled on democracy but confused with capitalism, and thus was successful, as processes go. Farmers who came from out of town to watch the horse or tractor pulls had to first pass the display of the Queen candidates' pictures, and on many evenings I would see a group of them standing thoughtfully in the small booth, hands in their pockets, their pants on fire with small change.

I lurked around the Queen's booth all fair week, sending out my most powerful ESP beams to everyone who entered: pick Melinda, pick Melinda, pick Melinda. This worked about half the time, but was useless against the thick-skulled, such as a dairy farmer named James who walked in every day and put a nickel in every can, causing me to slap my forehead in frustration. I couldn't imagine how a man who consistently canceled his own vote was able to manage a bunch of cows.

Of course my sister was the most beautiful girl anywhere, but as Saturday, the last day of the fair approached, I became sick with worry. What if there was cheating? (I didn't stop to consider that if any cheating had been done it would have been orchestrated by my father, so I had nothing to fear.) What if some other family had emptied a bank account into their daughter's can? It was a tough decision, but by noon I knew I had to do it. I broke open the yellow, plastic pig with the words *Farmer's State Bank of Mooreland* on the side and counted my loot. I'd been saving a long time. I had $1.61. I dropped the pennies into a burlap bank bag my dad had stolen and marched down to the fairgrounds.

Most of the cans were nearly full. The girl whose picture stood next to my sister's was fairly brimming. I took the lid off Melinda's can and poured in the whole of my liquid assets.

ON SATURDAY EVENING the gymnasium was teeming with excitement. All the girls sat on the stage in their lovely dresses, wearing corsages or carrying bouquets. The stage was decorated with lime-green Kleenex flowers, and a big square of poster board stuck to the front of the stage declared the title of the pageantry in words spelled out in glue and glitter. As her name was called, each contestant walked to the front of the stage, where Darryl Radford, the perennial emcee, asked her one question. For obvious reasons the questions were kept brief and manageable, like "What is your name?" and "Who is your sponsor this evening?"

Then my sister was called, and she walked up to Darryl in her white dress and black satin belt. She had made the dress herself. Her long, black, wavy hair shone in the stage lights, and her gray eyes were as round and lively as those of a cartoon princess. She and Darryl had known each other all their lives, and were fond of each other.

"Good evening, miss. Could you tell the audience your name?"

And all she said was "Melinda Kay Jarvis," but somehow her clear mind and her bright wit came through in her voice, and there was a very subtle little wavy shift in the audience, as if they had felt it. I sat in the front row, seven years old and beaming. *Nobody* deserved to win more than my sister. Nobody was as perfect and charming and irresistible. Nobody was as generous and true blue and good with stray animals. Nobody was as funny and sarcastic and miserable at home, scared of her father, desperate to get away, misused, overburdened, on the edge of tears all the time.

I crossed my fingers, prayed, tapped my foot, stuck my finger in my ear. I loved my sister so much I had even worn a dress for the occasion, which was making me perverse. The skirt was lined with some itchy netting, the collar was too tight, it was a pukey yellow color and smelled like mildew and wet coon hound. I had dragged the dress out of the back of the closet where it had formerly served as a bed for my cat Smokey and her five kittens. I was simultaneously regretting my insane loyalty and wishing I had also combed my hair and worn shoes when my sister was named first-runner-up.

Mary Murray began playing "There She Is" on the tuneless school piano and Darryl sang into the popping portable microphone as Carolyn, the girl whose picture stood next to my sister's in the judging booth, rose from her chair and walked unsteadily to the front of the stage, crying and clutching her heart. My sister stood next to her, graciously offering her congratulations.

The audience clapped heartily for Carolyn, whose blond hair and blue eyes were real crowd pleasers. I felt like I'd been punched in the gut. My sister was denied her title. An unworthy girl had won. The farmers liked Carolyn better than Melinda, and I had lost *a dollar and sixty-one cents,* the most money I'd ever had at one time in my life.

I don't remember much of what happened afterward until later in the evening, when someone came and found me near the merry-go-round, where I had just finished ripping the lining out of my dress and was desperately trying to stuff it in a trash barrel. There was a flurry of activity around the Band Boosters Food Tent. I could see my sister through the crowd, laughing with Astor Main, the Fair Board president and local undertaker, as he placed the gorgeous, much-coveted Fair Queen tiara on her head. For just a moment I had a chilling vision of my father taking the entire Fair Board hostage with his hunting rifle, which quickly evolved into him demanding a recount, during which it was discovered that Melinda had actually won by a hundred and sixty-one votes.

The truth was that just after the original crowning ceremonies, Carolyn admitted to one of her fellow contestants that she was three months pregnant, and was getting married in two weeks. Word spread like a field fire. With very little deliberation it was decided that Melinda, a girl of indisputable virginity, would hold the Fair Queen title.

Thus my sister became Fair Queen by default, and the next year in the Fair Parade I was allowed to ride alongside her in the back of the Queen's convertible, which bore the legend AN OLD-FASHIONED GIRL WITH AN OLD-FASHIONED SMILE, chosen just for Lindy by our clever mother. The handmade signs were taped to either door and surrounded by the ubiquitous flowers made of pipe cleaners and Kleenex. Melinda and I both wore high-necked Victorian dresses and Quaker bonnets and held parasols. Everything would have been perfect except that I refused to wear shoes, and so I had to sit very still and not swing my dirty, scabbed feet where they might be seen by the adoring crowd.

BLOOD OF THE LAMB

It wasn't enough for my mom to make me go to our Quaker church every Sunday; in addition, I had to listen to Batsell Barrett Baxter on television as we were getting ready to go.

Batsell Barrett Baxter was either an early example of a telepreacher or else an early example of Claymation. He had no live audience and no flashy suits. He sat dead still in a chair and spoke into the camera without ever moving his head or altering his blood pressure. More a scholar than an evangelist, he told his television audience about the Good News of

Jesus Christ with the same energy and enthusiasm that doctors generally reserve for discussion of really bad hemorrhoids. My mom loved him. Sometimes he even had "live" guests, other old and suited and clinically depressed men who had devoted their lives to God.

BBB: So. Dr. Brown.

DR. BROWN:

BBB: Your book, *New Life in the Old Testament*, just came out. Here it is. That's a nice cover. From Agape Press.

DR. BROWN: Yes.

BBB: Have you always been interested in the Old Testament?

DR. BROWN: Yes.

BBB: Why is that?

DR. BROWN: Well. Interesting that you should ask that question. I have always felt that . . . [there follows a pause so terrifying and extended that two corn crops fail] . . . our *roots,* as it were, as the people of the *cross,* begin with the *Hebrew* peoples—their fledgling relationship with . . . *God* . . . *;* their inability to abide by His *commandments;* their exile into *Egypt* and eventual passage into the *Promised Land* . . . Jesus Christ is, as it were, the *fulfillment* of the promises made to the Hebrew peoples in God's *first* covenant.

BBB: God's first . . .

DR. BROWN: That being the Old Testament, of course.

BBB: Of course.

My dad would have gotten up long before the rest of us, in order to do his mysterious middle-of-the-night stuff, which seemed to include standing in the yard with the dogs and looking up at the sky while drinking instant coffee so hot his upper lip was always a scalded red. Sometimes he went into his tool shed and moved things around, just a little. He whistled. By the time I got up, miserable and furious, it was still dark outside and his day was half done.

He watched Batsell Barrett Baxter with his arms crossed, his face lit up with a deep and sardonic amusement.

"Whoa. Amen," he'd say after a particularly bland but coherent point. Or my personal favorite, which he reserved for when my mom left the room: "You know, Zip: Batsell Barrett Baxter was born dead." Dad's insults made me laugh and groan at the same time, because they were absolutely indicative of the power of being grown up. I not only had to spend countless hours of my life worshipping a God I didn't believe in, I couldn't even complain about it, whereas Dad just sat down in his chair and called it as he saw it.

I HAD A FEW TRICKS to keep from leaving for church on time. I most often used the "I Can't Find My Other Shoe" tactic, and when that failed, "I've Lost My Little Pink New Testament."

"We're leaving!" my mom would call out, standing by the front door in one of the patched and remodeled dresses Mom Mary handed down to her. Sometimes she also wore a coat with three-quarter-length sleeves. Sleeves that stopped in the middle of her forearm! Go figure!

"I can't find my other shoe!" I'd shout back. "You go on without me; I'll be right there!" And then I'd dig around under the couch halfheartedly, surreptitiously pushing the lost shoe further and further out of my reach. Eventually, exhausted, I'd flop down on the couch in a sprawled position that suggested maybe I'd just spend the morning watching fishing shows with my dad, who would turn almost without turning and give me the one raised eyebrow look which contained the whole of his childrearing philosophy: "I respect every way in which you are a troublemaker, now get up and do what your mother says."

"Okay, okay, I'm going." Then I'd have to reach extra hard under the couch for my wayward shoe, sometimes giving myself a crick in the neck that would cause me to sprawl out on the couch again. I occasionally sprawled so long as to merit the thunderous *Zip!* warning which preceded any actual fury. Hopping on one leg, trying to squeeze my foot into a shoe that was inevitably too small, I'd look around the den frantically.

"Daddy! I can't find my little pink New Testament!" For reasons probably due to his own lack of churchiness, Dad believed me when I said I couldn't attend Sunday School without my Bible. I'm sure he thought of it as similar to attending fourth grade without a pencil.

The Little Pink New Testament device had worked long and well, so well that I thought of it as permanent. Then one Sunday morning, just as I was about to collapse on the couch in helpless surrender to my heathen fate, Dad reached down under his chair and pulled out my missing Bible.

"Where did you find that?" I asked, genuinely perplexed.

"In the bathroom trash can."

"You're kidding! How odd. I must have totally accidentally without even knowing it thrown it away with my old church bulletin last week. How silly of me!"

"Accidents happen," he said, handing it to me.

"You can say that again," I said, taking it from him as if with gratitude.

"But just to make sure this particular accident doesn't keep happening, I thought that from now on you could just give it to me when you get home from church, and I'll hold on to it for you. Then you'll always know where it is."

I sighed and headed for the front door. "Bye, Daddy," I said, not looking back at him.

"Don't sigh," he called out to my defeated back. "And don't dawdle."

WHEN I THINK of getting up for church, it is always winter in our house, but when I think of the actual walk, a small town block—our house and yard and the house and yard of Reed and Mary Ball, who never ever left their front porch—it is always a perfect summer day that will wither in my absence. I had to walk right past my bicycle, which sat in the yard as quietly and expectantly as a good horse; I had to ignore the hopscotch squares Julie and I had drawn on the sidewalk earlier in the summer, because hopscotching in a dress and too-small shoes was a recipe for disaster.

Sometimes the side of the house would exert a strange and supernatural magnetic force upon my body, which would cause me to fly up against it, face first, and stick there. With a great concentration of will I could rip one arm free, and then one leg, and eventually pivot until only my back was stuck. I was like a human fly, moving sideways. Smack, peel, peel, pivot, smack. I sometimes spent whole minutes just trying to pass one little section of the house.

Then there was the backyard, which I was morally obliged to inspect. Who, if not I, would notice a fallen nest; a broken hinge on the back screen door; the lost left leg of my big toothy doll named Jeremy? I stood in the center of the yard and turned around and around until my eyes were jittery, then headed for my dad's tool shed, a strange little wooden structure that was tilted decidedly north. The door was held closed with a wooden peg that turned, and inside was the most outrageous jumble of tools and chains and traps. The traps were all different sizes and hung from the ceiling and the walls and no way would I ever touch them. Everything in the shed was the exact same shade of gray, except for one little spot of color: my second-grade picture, propped up in the window. I was sporting the favored Pixie haircut and wearing a light-blue jumper my mother made, smiling a little closed-mouth smile that hid my toothlessness.

Stacked on the corner of the work counter were slabs of beeswax, which Dad rubbed on his hands before handling his traps. He coated the traps with it, too; it covered the human scent that might forewarn an animal of danger. My dad's relationship to the traps and the traps' relationship to the necks of certain animals was something best not considered too closely.

The beeswax, once a deep and satisfying yellow, had turned an earthy color. The little window through which Dad could look at Edythe's yard across the street was discolored. Whatever had descended over the whole of this shed was so powerful and complete it even had a smell, and not an unpleasant one. It was a combination of oil and metal, the wooden handles of heirloom tools, and the hides of rabbits and squirrels. I stood still and breathed deeply. I could smell a horse's tail, and bags of grain, long gone, that we fed to various ducks and rabbits who had come and vanished.

I could vaguely remember a horse named Princess who (could it be true?) was kept in this shed at night. There was just enough room for her to stand without moving, her tail against the wall and her head against the door. One winter morning my brother went out to feed her, and against all physical odds she had turned around in the night, and when he opened the door she reared up and kicked him with both hind legs, sending him flying across ten feet of yard and up against the side of the house. When we came running out to see what had happened, Dan was in a heap on the ground, trying to catch his breath. Two of his ribs were broken and his sternum was bruised. He wore a bright yellow, down-filled coat then, probably a color, like blaze orange, recognized by hunters. He was tall and muscular, but lean, and he unconsciously flexed his jaw muscles all the time, the way some people jingle the spare change in their pocket. Of my parents' children my brother fared the best, genetically speaking, and was in fact so handsome that both Mom and Dad were reluctant to take credit. Regardless of the fact that he was beautiful, and should have had every advantage because of it, the world was not right for my brother. There was some standard by which he measured everyone, all human activity, without articulating it or giving us any clue where we were going wrong. He was silent and furious nearly all the time. Girls were crazy about him.

The air in the shed was so thick and still I could almost hear it ticking. I could see, in a trick of memory, Princess's hind legs bursting out of the door of the shed; my brother flying backward, bent in the middle like a man accepting the momentum of a cannonball; his slide down the side of the house and his jumble of long limbs when he landed. An unexpected and corrosive dread overcame me, starting in my stomach. I felt like I was the meal over which two alligators were fighting, and all I could do was stand still and wait for one to win.

I have to go to church before Dad comes outside, I told myself repeatedly. *I have to go to church.* I stepped outside, blinking at the sudden brightness, like a person just emerged from a stint in solitary confinement. Between our house and Minnie Hodson's was our clothesline, which caught my eye. My mom had hung out a sheet patterned with fading yellow roses, two pillowcases, and a pair of her own underwear, which caused my sense of unease to billow. As I stood there looking at my family's laundry, Minnie Hodson slammed out of her own back door, followed by her spaniel dog, Lucky.

The two of them walked around the yard casually. It was a beautiful day. Minnie was feeding her chickens out of a pocket in the front of her apron, making little comforting clucking sounds at them, which they imitated. Lucky sat down smiling, his tail brushing a winged pattern into the dirt of the barren yard. I don't know how she chose, whether by some fixed criteria or just her own fancy, but suddenly Minnie reached down and picked up a chicken by the neck and spun it in an arc over her head, breaking its neck. Within seconds she had it on a darkened stump, where she cut off its head with a little hatchet she was carrying in the same apron.

She held the chicken's body upside down for just a few seconds, to drain some of the blood. Lucky surveyed the scene with a curious light in his eyes. I had unconsciously crossed part of the yard, and was now standing under the lower branches of the mulberry tree, still at an age where anything I couldn't see couldn't see me. The other chickens had scattered, and now Minnie and Lucky walked toward their back door. I grimaced against the inevitable screech when the door opened and its slamming shut, before they even happened.

And suddenly I felt my dad's hand on my shoulder. I looked up at him, at where he was standing in a corona of Sunday light, then back down at my shoes, which I had managed to stain with mulberries in the few minutes I stood absolutely still.

"What's going on out here?" Dad asked, crossing his arms and looking into Minnie's yard.

"Nothing, Daddy." I leaned over and spit on my old saddle shoe, then scrubbed at it with my fist. "I've got to get on."

He nodded at me, then turned back toward the house. If blood had a smell, he missed it; if something new and permanent was written on my face, no one was saying so. A cigarette burned in my father's hand everywhere he went.

SOMETIMES I GOT TO CHURCH during the silent time, which meant I could kiss slipping in unnoticed good-bye. But today Pastor Eddie was already preaching. Between the vestibule and the sanctuary were heavy, swinging doors on brass hinges, like those that lead to dining rooms.

I slid in next to my sister, who promptly reached out and pinched me on that wildly tender skin inside the upper arms. She knew I couldn't hoot or howl or even kick. All I could do was snort out a few breaths like a cornered cow.

Pastor Eddie was talking about Jesus, and how He died for all of us, to save us and cleanse us of our sins. God so loved the world, I was told again today, as I had been told incessantly throughout my life, that He sent His only Son to earth to serve as a sacrificial lamb. With Jesus's blood we were made whole; with His death we were set free. And all He wanted in return was our hearts, freely given. All we had to do was turn our lives over to Him. He was waiting right now. Wouldn't we come?

Pastor Eddie's eyes were closed and his arms were raised in a beseeching way. In the front row his wife, Shirley, who had made me the most beloved blanket I would ever own (and which I called my Shirley Quilt), had one hand clenched in the air, waving a tear-stained handkerchief. Around me there were choked whispers of "Yes, Lord," and "Oh, Jesus." Kathleen was at the piano, and began playing the chorus of "I Come" over and over, quietly.

The members of our meeting began responding to the altar call. My mom was one of the first to arrive, as usual. Soon nearly everyone was up there but me and one old woman who was too fat to walk. I had never been saved. It was a scandal. My sister periodically turned from the front of the church to give me stink eye, but I couldn't budge. I would never, ever go to the altar. Even when I tried imagining, as my Vacation Bible School teacher had urged me to do, my heart opening up like a lily to accept God's love, I felt nothing in my chest but my own stubborn, hard-beating muscle, not even remotely flower-like. If the Rapture came, as my brother threatened it was about to, I knew what my fate would be, and I was ready for it: I would be left with just my godless daddy and Minnie Hodson and her chickens, which we would take one by one, and kill, and eat.

UNEXPECTED

INJURIES

The people of Mooreland mostly took one of two kinds of vacations: they went to visit relatives in Tennessee, or they went camping. Some people liked to go camping even though their daily lives already resembled camping; once I saw two people honeymooning in a pup tent smack in the middle of the bride's parents' yard. The bride was a biggish girl, and as I passed the tent on my way to the post office,

I saw her bare feet sticking out through the flaps. I didn't think anything of it.

We didn't have any relatives in Tennessee, so we spent many weekends in various campgrounds around Indiana. My favorite was called Tall Trees, about ten miles from home. Tall Trees Campground was all the name implied and more. It had its own lake and an old wooden barn with a pool table and pinball machines. The campsites were not too close together, and the big building with the bathrooms and showers was usually clean and not an impossible walk away. I'd seen way worse. Once at church camp I went to take a shower in the middle of the afternoon and all the shower stalls had about an inch of water backed up in them, and every place I looked there were frogs. It was so much like an Old Testament plague that I nearly answered the altar call that evening, but instead just closed my eyes and said "Mickey Mouse" over and over until the feeling passed.

It took, quite literally, a whole day for my dad to prepare to go camping. The trailer had to be outfitted with supplies, and they all had to go in special tiny places, all facing the same direction; the truck had to be cleaned and gassed up and all the fluids checked and topped off; the hitch had to be stepped on seventy-four times to make sure it could handle the weight of the trailer; the trailer had to be connected to the hitch, which involved actually lifting the trailer off the ground and fitting it onto the ball. Sometimes an animal or a child might be standing too close during the crucial lifting of the trailer, the proximity of which could cause my dad to become his most godless. After the trailer was hooked up, my mom and I had to stand in the yard and signal to Dad in semaphore to

TURN ON YOUR RIGHT TURN SIGNAL. NOW THE
LEFT TURN SIGNAL. GREAT. TRY YOUR BRAKES.

Dad was convinced that tragedy was going to rain down on us
in the form of some bone-crunching accident, and all because one
of the wires connecting the trailer lights to the truck went out, so
sometimes we had to go through the whole light test four or five
times. Then the big side mirrors on his truck had to be adjusted for
ninety minutes. Then he had to drive the truck and camper around
the block a few times to make sure everything felt right. Generous
neighbors often stepped out of their houses and signaled that all
the lights were working as he went by. Finally, he would stand up
straight and sigh and say we were ready, and then I would get back
in the camper and off we'd go, driving less than an hour to the
campground, with me flying around in the back of the camper like
a little wayward piece of popcorn.

WE HAD A SERIES OF NEIGHBORS in the house to the north of
us after Minnie Hodson died; Petey Scroggs and his family lived
there for a while, and if I were able to visually represent Petey, the
portrait would be nothing but a cliché. He was a mean, short boy
with carrot-colored hair and freckles. His jeans were often twisted
around sideways and the collars of his striped T-shirts were always
stretched out and he had mean eyes and he ate his own fingernails.
Petey walked with the longest stride a short boy can afford, and
when he wasn't barreling down the sidewalk on his feet, he was
riding a very sinister-looking black bicycle that seemed to be made
of the Devil's own bicycle parts.

Petey got his looks from his mother, who kept her carrot hair in perpetual pin curls, by which I mean always in the pins. She and Petey were both a little cross-eyed, and she had a very high-pitched voice which caused my dad to call her Birdie. Petey looked and sounded just like her, even though he only came up to the waist of the housedress she wore all year long, which may have actually been an uncomfortable nightgown.

As for his smarts, Petey inherited those straight from his daddy, John, who was a mean drunk. My dad's nickname for John was Jethro, after Jethro Bodine from *The Beverly Hillbillies,* which seemed to me quite insulting to the real Jethro, who, while clearly stupid, was nonetheless charming and intended no harm. John was a tobacco-spitter. There was no end of mischief in his intentions. Once he raked up all the leaves in his yard, poured kerosene on them, and set them alight, right underneath the mulberry tree our two yards shared. Twice he had, while drunk, driven his car into the corner of his own house, and Dad had seen John set his own pants on fire while trying to light a match on the zipper of his fly.

In my loneliest hour I had no need of Petey Scroggs as a play-mate. I was, in fact, afraid of him, because of the many stories that circulated in Mooreland about his treatment of animals. He had once thrown a litter of kittens into a burning trash barrel, I heard at church, and Julie's aunt told me that he snuck into a woman's house while she was in the garden and plucked all the feathers off her parakeet, leaving it completely naked. And I knew in my heart with absolute certainty that he had been responsible for the kid-napping of my cat PeeDink one bitterly cold January.

When PeeDink didn't come home one night none of us was really worried, because his mighty hunting skills preoccupied him. Then he didn't come home a second night, and I had to go out in the dark and cold and call for him. After the third night we were all sore afraid, and we began canvassing the neighborhood, but no one could remember seeing him. Every day for a month I checked at Doc Austerman's clinic, in case somebody had accidentally turned him in as their cat, thinking that maybe they could get all the broken parts of him fixed, but every day the answer was no. I was nearly despondent without him. My dad finally sat me down one night and told me that I needed to accept that PeeDink was probably gone for good, because it was simply too cold for him to have survived longer than a few nights, especially given the fact that he was learning disabled. I cried and cursed God. I told Dad if he really loved me he would just go out and find him and bring him home, and day after day Dad tried, with no luck.

Then right at the end of January the weather turned so bitter that our water pipes froze and burst. Dad gathered up all the jugs he kept for just such emergencies and trudged over to the Scroggses' to borrow some water. While he stood in the kitchen watching Birdie fill the jugs, he heard a familiar, desperate meowing. He asked if the Scroggses had a cat, and Birdie said no. By this time Petey was in the kitchen, looking short and beady-eyed and nervous.

"Well, I believe I hear a cat somewhere," my dad said.

"No, you don't," Birdie shrilled, handing Dad his water jugs as quickly as she could.

"I believe the sound I hear is coming from the basement," Dad said, taking a step toward the basement door.

Petey skittered over like a greased pig, trying to insinuate himself between Dad and the basement. "Ain't no cat in here!" he squealed.

Dad quick thrust the water jugs into Petey's arms, who accepted them without thinking, and then Dad went for the basement door, which was so swollen he had to heave his shoulder against it to get it all the way open.

And into the kitchen sprang a soot-colored, howling apparition, nothing but ribs and a tail. Dad said that for a few seconds he couldn't honestly say whether it was PeeDink, until the cat looked up at him. At that moment there were three pairs of crossed eyes in one kitchen, which my dad later reported to be two too many for any man, so he grabbed the water jugs, thanked Mrs. Scroggs, and stomped out the back door, poor desperate PeeDink following close behind.

WHAT PETEY SCROGGS did to PeeDink was all the story I needed to know about him, but I hadn't yet reached the point of crossing the street to avoid him, or ignoring him in the hard snubbish way that means true enemies. So one afternoon, sitting in the backyard in the double glider my father won in a card game and lost two weeks later, I saw Petey walk across his backyard and into the barn where the Scroggses kept rows and rows of rabbits in cages. A few minutes later he came out with a big, fat white rabbit, and when he saw me watching him he raised his arm in a wave, and I waved back.

Mom and Dad were only a few feet away, going over my dad's camping checklist. My mom was having to do a lot of the work, because Dad had a maggot in his finger. A few days earlier he had slammed his hand in the door of the truck, eliminating nearly half an inch of his index finger, and the doctor had put a maggot inside the stump to eat the dead parts. Dad was a little crabby because he could feel it moving around.

It appeared that we were either twenty minutes or six hours away from leaving for Tall Trees, depending on whether my mom found three missing cans of sterno and a case of C rations Dad stole from the National Guard Armory.

"Bob," Mom said, throwing up her hands. "We have enough food for a *month*. Why do we need a case of C rations?"

"You never know."

Petey headed my way. He was carrying the rabbit with one hand under its belly and one hand holding the scruff of its neck. There was no fence separating our yards then, so he just walked over and sat down on the other side of the glider.

"You wanna hold my rabbit?" he asked, in his objectionable voice.

I don't know a sane person in this world who can resist a bunny. I nodded, and he passed his rabbit over to me, settling it in my lap.

It was a huge, furry sack of heat. I'd never seen a rabbit so big, or so white. Its skin hung down in folds on either side of my arms—it was in all ways bigger than my lap. I held it under the chin the way Petey had, with one hand, and rubbed its head with my other. Between the ears the rabbit's skull divided in the most delicate little dip. I felt it sniff my hand, moving its nose in that quick up and down way that is the subtle answer to *What does a rabbit say?*

I could have held it all day, but after only a few minutes Petey grabbed it by the neck and took off across the yard. I looked up into the setting sun and saw the outline of my dad moving toward me, then looked down and saw blood dripping on the tops of my blue tennis shoes. I looked up; I looked down; I could make sense of nothing I was seeing. Then both of my parents were sitting on the glider, and Dad had ahold of my hand, and I could see that there was a sizable, bunny-shaped portion of my index finger missing, and blood was running out steadily, dripping onto first my shoes, and then Dad's.

"Didn't you feel that rabbit biting you?" he asked, wide-eyed with disbelief.

"No," I said, thinking maybe he was a little sensitive because of his maggot. "I reckon I was hypnotized."

Dad looked at my mom, stricken. "She thinks she was hypnotized by a rabbit."

"Well, stranger things have happened," Mom said, carefully not looking at my dad's bandaged finger.

"Get in the house." Dad ordered me by pointing with his cigarette in the general direction of the living room window.

I got up slowly, cradling my bleeding finger. I deeply dreaded what was in store for me: much Ivory soap and hot water, followed by enough iodine to paint our front porch. No way would he settle for mercurochrome, either. We'd be lucky if he didn't go collect the head of the rabbit and send it to the game warden, just to be sure.

My sister came in the bathroom where I was sitting on the toilet lid, dejectedly waiting for Dad to collect sterile gauze pads and surgical tape.

"I didn't know rabbits were meat eaters," she said, looking at my bright orange hand.

"Petey's rabbits are." I still could not believe that a white bunny was capable of such carnage.

"Do you think he knew that rabbit was going to bite you?"

"I don't know why else he brought it over. I'm afraid we can't go camping now, too."

"You handle pain so well, sweetie," Melinda said, standing up.

"Well, I was hypnotized."

She walked out into the den, where Dad was still rooting through the medicine cabinet with his good hand. I heard her asking him about the camping trip, and his reply about how we'd be risking infection at every turn, including from the many, many bacteria that lived in the lake.

"What does Mom think?"

"I don't know. She's still out in the camper, counting Sterno."

Dad came in and bandaged up my finger until it was roughly the size of a lemon, then went out to begin the arduous process of uncamping. He found my mom sitting at the little table in the trailer, reading a book.

A few weeks later, while I was playing in the backyard, Petey and his much older brother, Billy, and their dad came barreling out of their house, John and Billy sounding huge and dumb and scary, Petey screeching around them importantly. I dashed around and hid behind my dad's tool shed, peeking my head out periodically to see what they were doing.

They each had a tool of some kind—I couldn't see clearly what the tools were—but all three of them looked dangerous. Petey

ducked into the barn and came out with a rabbit, which he handed
to his dad. John held it by the neck, then crossed its long ears at the
top, held them up to the side of the barn and stapled them there
with a staple gun. Billy stepped up with a wicked-looking little
hatchet, and whack! the rabbit's body was separated from its head,
which remained stapled to the side of the barn.

Headless bodies really do hop around for a couple seconds; this
was one of the indisputable lessons of Mooreland, Indiana. I saw
probably four or five such bodies bleed their life out and fall down
before my dad came out looking for me. By this time I was standing right out in plain sight, in roughly the same spot I had stood
just a year before, watching Minnie Hodson take the head off a
chicken for Sunday dinner. That patch of ground was a front-row
seat for nature's theater: years later I could stand right there and
look at the grave of a much-loved and long-lost dog.

Dad didn't stop to converse with me. He crossed our yard in
just a few steps, and before the Scroggs men even knew he was
there he had the hatchet out of Billy's hand and John up against the
bloody wall of the barn, Dad's left forearm hard against his throat.
Dad had on the face that no one in this world would choose to be
faced with.

"Do you See that Little Child standing in the yard watching
you, You Stupid Son-of-a-Bitch?!?" When pressed, Dad had a way
of emphasizing certain words that was like Winnie-the-Pooh gone
bad.

John was grinning in his shifty way, the way men smile at each
other when one has a hatchet and the other doesn't.

"I sure didn't see her there, Bob," he croaked out around Dad's
arm.

"You've got to Butcher your Rabbits on a summer afternoon when there are Children Outside Playing?!" Dad was spitting out every word.

"Now, I—" John started, but Dad stopped him.

"I've put up with enough out of you in the past two years, John, and now I'm going to draw the line: If you ever. Do anything like this again. I will tear off your arm. And shove it down your throat. Until you choke to death. Are we clear?"

John smiled stupidly. My dad was exactly the kind of man who made idle threats and then randomly acted on one. He had been known to raise a rifle, and to make peace over a bottle of whiskey. John knew better than to try to predict which he might do. He raised his hands in surrender.

"Sorry!" He called out to me. "Didn't see ya there! Won't happen again!" He looked like a clown.

Dad walked away quickly, and led me back into the house, roughly. "Go wash your hands," he said, as we went through the front door.

"But, Daddy, I didn't get—"

"Go wash them, I said." His fist was clenched tight on the doorknob. I washed my hands.

IT TOOK US LONGER than usual to get to Tall Trees, because twice I fell out of the top bunk with such a crash that Dad pulled over on the side of the road to make sure I wasn't broken, and then before we could pull back onto the highway we had to test the lights.

By the time we arrived I already had on my bathing suit, my

floppy shoes, and my Mickey Mouse sunglasses. My rubber nose-plug was hanging expectantly around my neck. We pulled into our favorite campsite and as soon as Dad shut off the engine I hopped out of the camper.

"Hey! Look! I'm all ready to go to the lake! Let's just all head down to the lake!"

But I ended up sitting on the picnic bench for the next hour picking scabs, as Dad planted us firmly and safely in our temporary home. Before I got anywhere near that bacteria-filled water he had built a fire ring, hooked us up to electricity, strung up the fishlights, smoked sixteen unfiltered Lucky Strikes, and made friends with the family at the next site. When he and I finally left for the lake, he had Mom going through everything in the camper, looking for the toothache kit he'd gotten in the Navy, back in 1954: just in case.

THE KINDNESS
OF STRANGERS

Our neighbor, Reed Ball, who never ever left his front porch, was a big old man who stood crooked, like maybe one of his legs was longer than the other. One day he wobbled down to the fence that separated our two yards and called out to my dad, who was working in our garden, that he was going to poison our dogs if they kept barking at night.

"Is that right?" Dad said, looking at Reed in an interested way.

"Damn right that's right!" Reed bellowed. He was another example of an old man who could barely contain his fury but also could never let it out.

"Keep you awake at night, do they?" Dad asked, leaning on his hoe.

"You know they do! They're not fit to kill!" He was talking about Kai, who was so highly evolved he could have been a spiritual leader, and Tiger. Poor Tiger. Anyone with even a little bit of a functioning heart would have pitied her, the way her snoot was shaped in such a way that she always sounded congested, and the fact that she was pig-shaped, and thus had no dignity.

"Reed. Do you ever go *in* your house? Because maybe if you slept *inside* your house you wouldn't be bothered by my dogs."

Reed made a sound like a gunked-up combustion engine then lifted and lowered one of his legs, probably the longer one, a gesture surely meant to convey stomping. He raised one of his gnarly old hands and pointed a finger at my dad.

"You mark my words!" he said, then turned and strode back to his house, up down, up down, up the steps and back onto the padded chaise lounge where he spent his whole life. His sweet wife, Mary, was sitting on the padded glider. No one had ever seen her move more than her arms and her neck. Dad watched Reed's slow progress, then waved at Mary in a neighborly way. She sweetly waved back.

Our dogs barked all night that night. They were highly perturbed about something. I finally got up and went outside with a flashlight to see what was bothering them; it turned out to be a bat circling a streetlight, eating dinner. I went inside their pen and sat down with them for a few minutes, trying to calm them down, but Tiger was so pleased to see me that she shimmied and yipped and snorted until I feared she would hyperventilate.

As I was closing the pen door to head back inside, I heard Reed call out from his porch, "You tell your dad I've had enough! This is the last time I'm going to tell him!"

"Okay, Reed," I yelled back. "Hello, Mary."

"Hello, sweetheart," I heard from the darkness of their porch.

THE NEXT MORNING I told my dad I was flat-out worried about what Reed might do to Kai and Tiger. Dad was casual, and said that he was working on it. He disappeared for a few hours, which was highly usual, and when he returned he was followed by a whole convoy of pickup trucks.

Dad came home at dusk, and parked in front of our house. All the other drivers just stopped wherever there was room and began unloading the cargo they were carrying in their truck beds. There were wooden crates and metal boxes and carriers obviously made at home. One kennel was large enough to house a healthy calf. I stood on the sidewalk for a few minutes watching them, then ran inside to get my mom.

"Mom! There's about two hundred hunter-looking men in our yard with Dad!"

Mom looked up from her book, granting me the unadulterated attention she usually reserved for really good science fiction.

"What are they doing?"

"They're . . . I don't know. There's a bunch of them and they've all got boxes full of dogs."

Mom slowly lowered her book and began the process of removing herself from the deep indentation in the couch that she had been carving into it over the past twenty years.

I ran back outside. Lined up all along the fence separating our yard from Reed's were crates filled with coon hounds, thirty-six by my count. They were nervous and jittery, pacing and circling. Some of them were already working themselves up into a howling lather. My dad walked back and forth in front of them, trying to calm the most disturbed. The dogs' owners left one by one without a word.

Mom cleared her throat behind me, and Dad and I turned around at the same time.

"May I ask?" She addressed Dad as if he had just made an announcement she found interesting, but not unexpected.

"Ask away," he said, shaking a Lucky Strike out of the pack.

"What, exactly, are you doing?"

"Dog-sitting."

"Dog-sitting. Are all of your colleagues going out of town at the same time?" My mom was patient as a saint, but she said the word *colleague* as if it were coated with the oil drained off a can of tuna fish.

"Yep, that's right," Dad said, inhaling deeply on his cigarette. He had a habit of blowing all the smoke out through his nose, like a bull. "They're going to a convention."

"Oh, a convention. Would that be for the Society of Drunken Philanderers?"

"The SODP, we call it," Dad said, nodding.

"I see." She stood still for a few more seconds, probably counting the dogs, then turned around and headed back toward the house.

"Give me a hand here, Zip," Dad said, uncoiling the hose, argument concluded. I helped him carry various buckets and pans out of his tool shed, which we filled with water and sat inside the kennels. The dogs were beautiful and stinky and hectic. From their pen, Kai and Tiger watched the proceedings without moving. Compared to these dogs, ours appeared medicated. I wasn't sure Tiger was even of the same species.

We finished with the watering, then stood back and watched the hounds try, without success, to settle down until they were called upon to perform the task for which they had been created. One blue tick who was exceptionally irritated chewed ceaselessly on the metal door of his cage; another couldn't stop scratching his ear.

"Daddy," I said, reaching up to scratch my own ear, in sympathy. I would need a flea dip before the night was over. "Who _were_ all those men?"

"Aw, I don't know, honey," he said, flipping his cigarette into the gooseberry bush.

"You mean they're not your friends?"

"Nope. I'd never seen them before. They're good people, though."

"Well, how did we end up with their dogs?" I asked, completely mystified.

"Word gets around when a man needs help," he said. He took my hand and we headed toward the house. At the time I thought he meant that he was helping a group of men he didn't know, but I quickly realized that the opposite was true.

I GOT TO STAY UP late that night. I didn't make a peep about it, but just kept sitting on the couch next to my mom like I was used to the nightlife. It got completely dark outside, and then darker than that, and then the moon rose up and silvered the yard, and just when I was about to fall asleep against Mom and my own better judgment, another truck pulled up in front of the house, and Dad stood up as if he'd been waiting.

Mom didn't say anything and I didn't say anything. I just climbed down off the couch and pulled my red galoshes on over my pajamas and followed my dad outside. He shook hands with the driver, who was tall, shy, and looked like he might have a tapeworm.

"This ought to do it," the man said, handing Dad a smaller crate. I couldn't see what was inside it, but Dad held it away from his body.

"Tell Ron I sent my thanks," Dad said, walking toward the backyard.

"Not a problem," Lanky Man said, climbing in his truck like a marionette.

I galoshed as fast as I could after Dad, and the dogs and I realized at the same moment that what Dad was holding was a raccoon. If I'd been any less a child I would have wet my pants from the sound the dogs made, collectively; one of them barked so hard and furiously that he tipped his kennel over, and he never stopped barking as he somersaulted inside it. Twice Dad lost control of the crate holding the raccoon and nearly dropped it, which would have resulted, of course, in the raccoon running right up my pajama leg to bite me in some tender place and make me rabid. I was so overcome by the commotion and the potential for disaster that I had to just sit right down on the sidewalk and put my head between my knees.

I looked up and saw Dad gently setting the raccoon down in the middle of the yard, about twenty feet from the row of kennels. By this time the dogs were hysterical, throwing themselves against cage doors and leaping up and smacking their bony heads, repeatedly. When I was sure that none of them would actually escape, I walked out and joined my dad at the epicenter.

"That raccoon is gonna have a heart attack," I shouted. Lights were coming on all over Mooreland, everywhere except Reed and Mary's house. "It must be scared out of its wits."

"That's one way to look at it," Dad said, glancing at the dogs and then at the raccoon, as if he were watching a tennis match.

"What's the other way?"

"Well, this is the luckiest night of this particular raccoon's life. There's no chance it'll ever come across thirty-six caged coon hounds again."

I nodded. After a few minutes Deputy Jim drove up next to our house slowly, with his lights off. He stepped out of his cruiser and stretched, then moved his head from side to side to pop his neck. He was wearing his pajamas and his deputy hat.

Dad walked over to the car and talked to Jim for a few minutes. The dogs never slowed down. They would have barked and howled and heaved as long as they had oxygen. Jim took off his hat to scratch his head, and Dad said something that caused him to guffaw and bounce his forehead up and down on the roof of the car. Next to me the raccoon seemed to be having a seizure. I tried to make out its features in the moonlight, but it was just one big panicky fur ball. By this time Johnny Scroggs was standing in his yard watching the proceedings, and Edythe, who never slept at night anyway, had decided it was a good time to play the piano. She was banging away at "When the Roll Is Called up Yonder," and whistling. My sister came over with a lawn chair, then sat down and started brushing her hair. My mom was conspicuous by her absence.

Before the night was over half the town had gathered in our yard, as if we were hosting a fourth of July picnic. Sometime before dawn Dad carried the raccoon, who was clearly permanently damaged, over to the bed of his truck and drove it out to the woods at the edge of town. The dogs continued howling for about ten seconds after he left, then collapsed into dog heaps and fell asleep. Throughout the conflagration there had been no sign of Kai and Tiger, neither hide nor hair, as my Mom Mary would say. They had stayed safely tucked in their dog houses, silent.

By the time Mom and Melinda and I got up for church the next morning, all the dogs were gone. Dad was already out in the garden, watering his fruit trees. I slipped on an old dress that had lost its hem; my gym socks and saddle shoes; grabbed my little pink New Testament from where Dad kept it on his end table, and told Mom I'd meet her at the corner.

I reached Dad at the same moment Reed reached the fence. Dad said hey to me, then looked up at the sky as if he'd just realized it was morning.

Reed cleared his throat so long and ferociously I feared one of his lungs had worked its way loose. "Pretty funny," he finally said, without laughing.

"What's funny?" Dad said, turning off the hose.

"You know what I'm talking about." Reed bit off the end of every word, like a drill sergeant.

"Nothing funny happening over here, that I can see," Dad said, wrapping the hose in a loop between his elbow and his hand. "It's just another Sunday morning with me, Not Fit To Kill and Not Fit To Kill, Jr."

In the yard Kai was lying on his back looking up at a cloud that was shaped like a daisy and Tiger had just tipped over sideways after chasing her own butt for ten straight minutes.

"Hmmph." Reed snorted. It sounded like a thunderstorm that lost the nerve to strike.

Dad looked down at me. "Aren't you supposed to be in Sunday School?"

I nodded. "I'm on my way. I'm meeting Mom at the corner."

"Go on, then," Dad said, carrying the hose back to the shed. "But don't you cross that street."

"Dad," I moaned, collapsing in the middle like an old balloon. "There aren't even any cars to watch for."

"Don't kid yourself," he called back over his shoulder. "There's danger everywhere."

Reed closed his eyes for a moment, leaning against the fence, then sighed and began to clomp back toward his porch. He wore the same thick, heavy shoes my dad had to wear at Delco Remy, the factory where they had both worked, and the seat of his brown pants was shiny. I hated the feeling old people aroused in me, especially when they were eating so carefully and patiently, or when they were waiting for someone, or at times like this, when they were working so hard to get from point A to point B. I wanted to just quick take the situation in hand and make it better—*here, give me that spoon*, or *climb on my back, I'll just carry you home*—but it also made me want to kick something and bite myself.

I swallowed, rubbed the nubbly outside of my Bible, then skipped out of the garden and began to hopscotch past Reed and Mary's house. Reed was just stepping up onto the porch, slowly making his way back to his chair. As I passed them I called out, "Hey, Reed! Hey, Mary!"

And Reed took the time to turn all the way around and wave at me, and Mary called from the glider, "Hello, sweetheart."

FAVORS FOR
FRIENDS

Some families had lived in Mooreland since before it had a name; those families lived in their houses the way the rest of us live in our skin. But Minnie Hodson's house couldn't seem to hold anyone for very long. The years Petey Scroggs lived there I felt like I walked under a dark cloud, and then the whole rabbit-butchering bunch of them left, and the sun came out in a crazy bright spring, because

Andy Hicks and his family became my neighbors. There were eight Hicks children, which was a lot even by Mooreland's standards, and they were all excellent, but Andy was my favorite.

There are people in this world so perfect that the fact of them feels like a personal gift, and Andy was one of those people. Here are some perfect things about Andy: 1) He could be funny for a whole solid day without ever once being stupid, and one time during lunch he made me laugh so hard a noodle came out my nose. 2) He took me to the park to explain the facts of life to me. We were on the swingset, and what he told me was so graphic and so utterly wrong that I had to stop swinging; get sick; go home and not speak to my parents for three days because I feared they had done a particular thing that was known only by initials. Then I went to my friend Rose's house and passed the information on to her, and her mother stopped speaking to my mother for three days. 3) Down the street from us lived a redheaded bully named Eddy Lipscomb, who was forever threatening to look at my panties. Andy wrote a song about him:

Eddy Spaghetti with the meatball eyes;
Put him in the oven and make french fries.

4) Andy was tall and blond and soft and kind of girly, and nothing like Eddy Lipscomb. 5) He could sing like the main singer of God's own singing angel band. He could sing any kind of song, and would sing anytime I asked, even if we were walking down the street. Sometimes he just stood up in Friends Church and started to sing, and it was nothing but religious. His singing almost always

made me feel happy and sad at the same time, but sometimes it was so beautiful that I just got mad, like once at the Mooreland Fair Talent Show, when it hit me especially hard and I decided to make him forget the words through mind control so he would stop singing, and he forgot the words and stopped singing and then I wanted to die.

When Andy came over one afternoon in August and asked if I would be willing to take care of the Hickses' old dog, Jiggers, for a week, while the family went to visit relatives in a holler in Tennessee, I was thrilled to say yes. The last song I had heard Andy sing at church began "Feed my lambs, my son / Feed my sheep." There was nothing about me that made me deserve a friend like him, and I wanted to feed his sheep.

I STOOD ON THE sidewalk outside the Hickses' house, waving to them as they drove away in their massive station wagon. I was generally trying to look responsible. The Hicks parents, Homer and Loverline, had somehow fit all eight of the children and at least a little bit of luggage into that one car, and the rear bumper was so close to the ground that sometimes sparks flew up.

When I turned around, Jiggers was still standing in the yard in exactly the same position she had been ten minutes before, her brown head bowed down by the long-term effects of gravity. It seemed that controlling her bladder was her one, overwhelming priority, because sometimes a little bit of pee would start to come out and she would look sad and shut it off and stand and stand and stand, and then a few minutes later a little bit more pee would come out. It was steambath hot that day, and she couldn't even muster up the strength to pant, which made me worried, because as I understood it, dogs did all their breathing through their tongues.

I walked over to her and patted her on the head. Her fur was so soft it was like something already leaving this world. "Jiggers, honey, why don't you just let all your pee out and then go lay down in the shade?" She looked up at me with her filmy eyes, which had once been brown, but were turning a milky blue. She moaned some, then shuffled over to the shade and lay down.

I sat down beside her. I wasn't at all certain what was required of me as a dog-sitter. I knew I was supposed to give her food and water, but was that all? Obviously we were not going on any brisk walks; we weren't going to play fetch; she certainly was not going to get me out of any life-threatening scrapes. When she plopped her head down and started to snore I decided to leave her be. I checked her food and water dishes, which were both full, and went on my way.

What with bicycle rodeo and some general town duties, I didn't get back to check on Jiggers until it was dark, and then I couldn't find her anywhere. Her dishes were still full, but she didn't come when I called, and it was too dark for me to do any Indian tracking.

I ran home to my dad. He was sitting in his chair watching *Bonanza* when I burst through the door.

"Dad! I can't find Jiggers! She's nowhere to be seen and won't come when I call!"

"She's probably sleeping under the porch," he said, without looking up from the television. "I'd get under the porch if I was Jiggers. It's hotter than billy-be-doggone bangtree outside."

"What does that stupid sentence mean, anyway?" I asked, sitting on the floor beside his chair. Everyone in my family said it except for me, because I had some standards.

"How can you say it's stupid if you don't know what it means?" he asked, giving me the one eyebrow.

"Okay, what does it mean?"

"I don't know." He turned back to the television.

"Aaaahh! Then where did you hear it?"

"From Mom Jarvis. I suspect you'd better take it up with her."

"Mom Jarvis is dead! I never saw her in my whole life!"

"Don't ask her, then. Ask your mother."

"Don't ask me," my mom said from the corner of the couch.

"Do you even know what we're talking about?"

"No. Just don't ask me." She was reading *Stranger in a Strange Land* for the sixteenth time.

"Now, Zippy: have I ever told you the origin of the saying 'slicker than snot on a doorknob'?" Dad asked, causing me to fall over laughing. And thus I comfortably forgot about Jiggers, and went to bed without thinking about her again.

THE NEXT MORNING I looked in on Jiggers and saw nothing, and that afternoon and that night the same, and the third morning following the Hickses' departure I was feeling a bit fluttery in my stomach, and by that night, when there was still no sign of her, I was basically panicked. When I went home that night Dad asked, incorrectly, if Jiggers had plenty of food and water and I said, honestly enough, that she did.

When Andy had been gone four days a distinctive smell began to hover around his house. On the fifth day it was strong enough to keep me from opening their gate, and on the sixth day customers at Newman's Marathon began to complain, and gasoline still had *lead* in it.

The truth of the situation was not lost on my dad, and a certain binding sheepishness grew up around us. I didn't know what to do, and he knew what to do but couldn't do it, and it became clear that our relationship was simply not forged out of confrontation.

THE HICKSES CAME HOME late on a Saturday night. I was lurking like a bandit around the gas pump farthest from their house, periodically covering my face with my favorite T-shirt, which had printed on the front a large-mouth bass leaping up out of a lake.

The ten of them got out of their station wagon, one after another, slowly, as if out of a clown car at a very sad circus. Faced with the meeting of the two elements—the actual dead dog and the actual family—I could only smash my face up against the cool glass of the gas pump until my nose hurt. I kept thinking of how long my friends had Jiggers in their life; how she had been their family dog for as long as some of the little Hickses had been alive, and how I would have felt if we had lost Kai this terrible way, because of a stupid little neighbor girl who didn't even know how to dog-sit.

Homer walked over to me in his exceedingly slow and shambling way and asked in his slow accent what happened.

"I think Jiggers must have tore her stomach on a sharp rock crawling under the porch, Homer, it was hotter than . . . it was so *hot* the whole time you were gone," my voice was just a wretched little squeaky whisper, and I couldn't seem to peel my face off the gas pump.

Homer had a high-pitched, breathy mountain voice, as gentle as a time that will never come again, and he turned to his eldest son, Chris, and told him to go fetch a blanket and a flashlight, and then he did the unthinkable. He crawled under the porch where the smell was nearly visible, and wrapped Jiggers's body in an old blue blanket and dragged her out, and then he and his sons set to silently digging a grave in the backyard, under the shade of the mulberry tree we shared. It seemed to take hours. I stood out by their gate the whole time, fierce tears burning my face. When Jiggers was completely covered, all the Hicks men stood up and leaned on their shovels, and Andy began singing "Poor Wayfaring Stranger." His voice was sweeter than grief, and the last note of the song hovered so long I couldn't bear to leave the front gate, even after all the Hickses had gone inside and begun getting ready for bed. Homer saw me there when he came to turn off the porchlight, and ambled out to me.

He stood before me quiet for a minute, and then his big hand covered the top of my head.

"We all want to thank you for taking such good care of Jiggers. She was an old dog, and it must have been a comfort to her to have you near her at the end."

I could only nod, and then I took off running for home, wiping my face on my fish shirt as I went, so that no one would ask any questions. But when I ran in the door my dad barely looked up from his program and my mom just waggled her fingers at me from around her book, and I knew Dad would never mention Jiggers again, not her life or her death or her grave.

THE HICKSES DIDN'T COME to church the next day, but Loverline's two sisters, Ernestine and Deltrice came, and they stood up and spoke about what a blessing it was to visit the home place with all their family gathered around them, and how we only know God through our relationships with his children, and when they sat down we all felt closer to Jesus, except for me, because I thought the whole idea was a bunch of crap.

I didn't see Andy that whole week, because I mostly hid in my house, and then the following Sunday I wore some gorgeous plastic fingernails to church, and a little ways into the silent time Andy slid into the pew next to me. I couldn't bear to look at him. He took a pencil out of his pocket and wrote on the church bulletin: "Don't you have the most beee-yuuuu-ti-ful hands?!" And I wanted to write back so many things, but it was time to start singing, and when Andy opened his mouth, I knew absolutely that this was not one of the mourning days, but one of the rejoicing.

HAUNTED HOUSES

Julie and I had pitched a pup tent in my front yard, right next to the fence where we very first met when we were three years old. We were lying on our bellies looking through binoculars at Edythe's front door; Edythe, the evil old woman who had lived across the street from me my whole life. Edythe, who appeared to be immortal.

My binoculars were from the Mickey Mouse Club, and I knew that they were absolutely, inarguably intended for moral purposes, such as Finding Hurt Or Lost Things, and that the Mouseketeers might be unhappy to find me using them to Spy On An Old Woman, but I had to keep a safe distance from her.

Julie's binoculars were great big and professional, and came in a crumbling leather case that left brown streaks on our hands. We had swiped them off Julie's Granny, who was all the time forgetting where she put stuff anyway. If necessary, we were both prepared to swear on the Holy Bible that Granny had given them to us and then forgotten. This was, I very well knew, a shameful use for a Bible.

I don't know how long we'd been lying there watching Edythe's door, but it must have been forever. Julie was getting cranky because we'd forgotten to bring candy bars, and I was feeling the beginnings of about six hundred chigger bites in the waistband of my shorts. I was about to give up when Edythe's front door opened, causing my throat to close so tightly that my breath came out in a little whistle.

We snapped our binoculars into a locked position, and as soon as I stopped wheezing I told Julie what I had learned about Edythe since our last reconnaissance mission.

"My sister says she eats a stew made out of puppies."

Julie turned and looked at me for just the briefest second. "Nuh uhn," she said, but in a way that was like she wanted to hear more. Edythe was standing on her front stoop, looking up at the sky and withholding her approval.

"Melinda says she takes the puppies when they're at their cutest, when they've got all that extra skin, and just tosses them in a pot of boiling water with some carrots, and that's her dinner."

We watched Edythe in silence for a few moments as she walked imperially down her sidewalk on Broad Street, her hands clasped together behind her back, her massive shelf of a chest thrust forward, her stride that of a field marshal about to bestow a visit on the degraded troops.

"Let me tell you something else, Julie," I whispered. "I've been counting the number of days in a row she wears that same dress, and she's up to twenty-three."

"Whoo," Julie said.

WHEN I TOLD MY MOM about the puppy stew she just said pshaw. I asked her wasn't it a fact that Edythe was all the time trying to kill my best cat, PeeDink, and she said Edythe just didn't like cats in her yard, and that PeeDink always got away safely. I asked her wasn't it true that at our last church picnic Edythe had brought cookies that appeared to be covered in snot?

"Now you're just being ridiculous," Mom said, trying to shoo me outside.

"What were they made of, then?"

"Well. I'm sure I can't say. But only because I didn't taste them."

"Ah ha! You didn't taste them because they came out of Ede's nose, that's why!"

My mom snorted. "You're shameless. We should feel nothing but pity for that old woman."

"Pity?!" Now this got my goat, as Mary Ball down the street was fond of saying. "Is it or is it not true that that 'poor old woman' tried to kill me in my baby bed?"

For just a moment Mom looked like she would acquiesce, then

pushed me out the front door instead. "That was a long time ago. You've got to learn to let go of things, honey, or at least stop bringing them up. She's a very troubled person."

I WAS CONVINCED Edythe ate puppy stew in order to give her the strength to put spells on people. I thought this because my sister had also mentioned, in passing, that if Edythe got me in a hard-core eye-lock she could draw me right into her house, which was unimaginable. When I pressed for the details of what Edythe would do to me once she had me, Melinda became uncharacteristically silent.

"Tell me! I have to know! I have to know how to protect myself!"

"Well, sweetheart," she began, while gently trying to press down a clump of my gravity-defying hair, "you know she hates all of us, but especially you. There isn't really anything you can do."

I felt the urge to shimmy up my sister's body like a panicked little monkey. "Why?!" I wailed. "Why does she hate me so much? I've never done anything to her!"

"She hates you because she and Mom used to be best friends, and then you came and broke up their friendship by demanding so much attention. Also she just hates little kids. But especially babies. Especially you."

I sat down in the yard, defeated. Half of my butt was falling into a big earthworm hole I'd dug in the middle of the night. I was excellent at catching earthworms. I had my own grub box and everything, and sometimes when I went fishing with my dad we'd have so many worms left over I'd just toss them out to the fish, like dessert.

"But didn't she know I was going to get born when Mom was pregnant for me? Couldn't they have just worked something out then?"

Melinda looked off into the distance, still patting the top of my head.

"What? Lindy. What."

"I don't think I should be the one to tell you."

"Aaaaahhhh! Tell me what?!" I knew from Marcus Welby, M.D., that this could and did sometimes happen, that bad news was followed by more and more bad news, until finally the doctor was telling you that you had to give up coffee, which I knew for a fact would have killed my dad.

"Mom doesn't want you to know yet, but I think you're old enough." She paused for dramatic effect, as my heart leaped around in my chest like a bluegill on a line. "You're adopted. Mom was never pregnant for you."

I had to lie straight down in the dirt. Oh, my god. This explained so many things. I couldn't think of any right offhand, but I knew my life was about to become tragically clearer to me.

When the sky stopped twirling I jumped up and ran straight in the house to my mother, who was sitting in her corner of the couch, which by this time was a total nest. She was reading Isaac Asimov, the love of her life, and eating popcorn from the night before.

I skidded to a stop in front of her and gave her a look of hardest accusation. Without looking up at me she said, "You should brush that worm stuff off before you come in the house."

"As if that matters! How could you not tell me I was adopted?!

Don't you think I have a right to know? And who were my real parents anyway?" I was trying to be mature, but periodically spit flew.

"Gypsies, honey." She had still not looked up from *Isaac Asimov Explains the Whole of Reality and Then Some*.

"Gypsies? Really?" This was somewhat compelling. I sat down.

"Yes, I thought we managed a very wise trade."

"Gypsies? In Mooreland?"

"They were just passing through. We heard them long before they arrived, because their horses and their wagons are all covered with bells. It's quite lovely. And they were led into town by a pack of wolves, who, during the full moon, stand up and preach." She looked up for a moment, remembering. "They were such a sight."

There were at least forty-two questions I needed to ask, but only one that really mattered. "What did you trade for me?"

Mom looked at me lovingly. "A green velvet bag."

"A velvet bag?! Who wants a stupid bag?"

"Well, it was a very special bag. It had no bottom."

"Ha! Joke's on them!" I had to tip over a little for laughing at the retarded gypsies, then straightened back up as I realized I was laughing at my own family.

"Oh, it *looked* like it had a bottom. It looked just like a normal bag, except that you could just keep putting stuff in it. It was like the human heart, sweetie: there was no end to what it could hold." My mom insisted on saying such things, even though almost no one understood what she meant. My dad sometimes called her Addlebrain because she read so many books.

"If you had such a great bag"—its uses escaping me for the moment—"then why did you trade it for me?"

"The gypsies were camped out down at the school playground, and one night your dad and I were drawn by the preaching wolves. And just before we left, we peeked inside one of the wagons, and there you were, lying on a sheepskin rug in a pool of lantern light. And we took one look at you and it was just like falling in love."

"Ugh." I made a little throwing-up face.

She picked up a few pieces of popcorn and looked back down at her book. "Plus, you were born with a tail."

I looked at her, completely speechless, my mouth hanging open exactly like a creature with a tail.

"We had it removed so your pants would fit. Also we didn't want you to suffer in school."

I jumped up and headed for the door. "Okay, thanks, that's good enough for me, I'm just going to go outside for a minute and . . ."

My sister was rocking back and forth very gently in the porch swing, studying her lines for *Up the Down Staircase*.

I stood on the front step for a moment, contemplating the news. Mom and Edythe had been best friends because they both read books and they were both basically insane. I had heard from the Hickses, who had stayed close to both Edythe and mother, that the two of them had had some very interesting conversations before I came along. Okay. And then Mom and Dad picked me up from the gypsies and Mom had to tend to me, plus there was all the trouble of having my tail removed, and Mom and Edythe couldn't talk as much anymore, and Edythe got really mad and jealous and tried to smother me in my baby bed while Mom was sweeping the front porch, but Mom had a premonition and ran in and caught her and then chased her across the street swinging the broom at her, screaming like a banshee, whatever that was. And Edythe had gone on hating me just as much as the day I arrived in the caravan, and nothing would ever stop it, unless she could lure me into her house with the evil eye and squeeze my thumbs. The story snapped itself clear in my mind, like a mousetrap. The most important thing of all was, of course, that I was a gypsy.

"Did she tell you?" Melinda asked, still looking at her play.

"Oh. Yeah, she told me." And I stepped off the front porch and headed for the drugstore for a lemon phosphate. I took my gypsy blood and my tail and walked right past Edythe's house instead of crossing the street like I always did, in order to show my sister a thing or two, but just as I reached the edge of her yard, Edythe stepped out her front door whistling and I had to take off running for my life, even though I was wheezing so hard I saw stars.

THE DRUGSTORE WAS OWNED and operated by a man named, no kidding, Doc Holiday. It had a tin ceiling that must have been twenty feet high, and old wooden ceiling fans. There was a marble counter and twisty black iron stools and a soda fountain. The candy cases were made of oak and curved glass, and the doors slid open on ball bearings, delicately ticking. In the back of the long, rather narrow store were booths and tables where kids carved their initials and left their old chewing gum, and the west wall was all shelves of medicines and toiletries. My mom said that some of the medicine was so old it had undoubtedly come over on the Ark.

There was a magazine stand, and a twirling rack that held comic books.

Many people found Doc Holiday's personality objectionable, but I appreciated how one always knew where one stood with him, which was too close and making too much noise. He never even looked at people as he shouted at them, which was also reassuring to me, as if he were actually yelling at someone on the other side of the front window, or into the rear bathrooms. Doc dressed like a pharmacist, but asking him for advice was a mistake. I was once in the drugstore when a woman asked if Bag Balm was good for diaper rash.

"I don't know! What are you asking me for?!" he bellowed, looking north.

Doc was not in the Rx business, nor was he in the business of meddling in other people's affairs. He didn't step into fights or defend small children from bullies. The bottom line for me was that I wasn't safe in his establishment, not from any fate that might befall me, and particularly not from Edythe. At the Marathon station all the Newmans and all of their mechanics were on full alert when I was there, and would tell me exactly where Edythe was if they saw her approaching, and Big Dave had even figured out a way for me to climb into a little filthy tool closet if it looked like she was actually coming into the station. At the post office I had once tried to climb right inside our tiny mailbox when Edythe came in behind me, and from that time on the postmaster, Ralph, had let me hide behind the Dutch door leading to the mail-sorting room when necessary.

But Doc Holiday, who wore bowties and suspenders and had a perfectly round, bald head, and who in all ways appeared to be a

That if you monkey around with sin
It'll make a monkey out of you!

"That's a very nice song. Thanks."

"You're welcome."

He was doing something under the hood that required that he study a certain place for a really long time, and then take a ratchet and turn it and turn it while making little huffing noises, and then study and study some more. When my dad concentrated really hard he chewed on the side of his tongue, which I knew and he didn't and I wasn't about to tell him.

"Daddy, do you think Edythe knows I ain't really a Christian?"

"Don't say ain't. I don't know. She sees you in church three times a week, doesn't she?"

"Yessir."

"Well, I'm guessing that she thinks of herself as a Christian because she's there, so she probably thinks you are because you're there. See what I mean?"

"Even though it ain't true?"

"Don't say ain't. Most people don't care if it's true or not, as long as you're sitting there with your money in your hand for the offering."

"Well, she for sure knows you're not a Christian because you don't even go and pretend."

He ratcheted a minute, grunted, stopped, and studied. "Oh, Edythe always hated me, even when she and your mom were so thick. And I never liked her, either. She used to call our house and pretend she was going to commit suicide if your mother didn't run over there every evening. One night she called and said she drank a whole bottle of iodine. I knew she didn't, but I called an ambulance and told them that she had, that she would deny it with her dying breath, and that they needed to just go ahead and pump her stomach, and they did."

"You did not!"

"I did. And she never forgave me, either, nasty old bat."

I stood looking at Edythe's yard. PeeDink just wouldn't stay out of it, and every day she went hunting him with her rake. I couldn't even imagine how sweet my life would be if someone would just come along and haul that old woman on down the line.

Dad was looking at me. "Are you going to talk to me all day?"

"I might."

"Well, don't. I'm about to lose my temper and start cussing, so go find something to do."

"Okay, then. See ya, Daddy."

"Take care, Zip."

I TOOK OFF ON my bicycle. I intended to head down to the post office and play a little rodeo. There was a ramp that led to the back door, about three feet off the ground, and Julie and I could ride up it full speed and go right off the end. For about a year we'd been having some good times in that parking lot.

I was almost there when I passed Ruth Huff walking down Broad Street with her hideous old collie, King. She waved. I waved back.

I decided to ride around the block and give some thought to Ruth Huff. Now she was as old as Edythe, easy, and just as disgusting. In fact, I believed they shared the same dresses. And she lived in a huge, falling down, scary haunted house that didn't even have any lights, on a lot right next to our church. There were cats swarming all over that house, like bugs. Nobody knew how she fed them. And she walked around town all day, every day, with King, who was five hundred dog years old and was just one big clump of matted fur, except on his snoot and around his butt, which were both naked. King could only pant and gasp for air. He never had a good day, as far as oxygen went.

I passed Ruth again. She waved. I waved.

Ruth also went to my church, and like Edythe, she had a powerful stink. All the stinky old people went to my church. Ruth maybe even had double the odor of Edythe, because of all the cats and the constant presence of King's mange. She carried a little black-beaded purse with her everywhere she went, which looked like she'd been carrying it since Christmas Eve of 1872, and in it she kept a plastic baggie filled with quarters. No one knew what they were for.

When I approached Ruth again, she waved me over. Her hands were all gnarled up, and dirtier than Edythe's.

I rode up next to her, then leaned over and very reluctantly patted King on top of his head, where I could completely feel his bony skull. On impulse I checked the sky for buzzards, but it appeared that King would escape for another day.

"How are you, angel?" Ruth asked, patting me on the arm with one of her claws.

"I'm fine, ma'am, and how are you?"

"You're a Jarvis, am I right?" One of her rheumy eyes was looking at the post office.

"That's right."

"You're the little Jarvis?"

"I'm the baby of the family. I've been seeing you in church my whole life, ma'am."

"Well." She nodded, as if a great mystery had been solved. "You want a quarter?"

"Oh, no—" but she was already scrambling in her purse.

"Here you go, take it."

When she handed it to me I was filled with the spooks about her dirty fingernails touching me, and there was something in the moment that seemed to make it hang suspended. One of Ruth's eyes was looking right at me, and the quarter was touching my hand; one of her fingernails was just grazing my palm, and even King had raised his head for the transaction. Everything was going wrong for King except whatever was behind his eyes, because when I glanced at him I saw nothing but smarts.

I rode away, toward the drugstore. I always kept a penny in my shoe. I turned back and waved at Ruth. She waved.

THERE WERE SO MANY animals buried in our backyard that every time we planted a tree or rototilled the garden a handful of smooth white bones got churned up into the light. It was disturbing. We were only allowed by law to bury animals under a certain weight, but everyone defied the code.

For instance, when Big Dave Newman's most beloved horse, Navajo, died from eating a piece of barbed wire fence, we left him lying where he was until the middle of the night, then we all snuck out and helped drag him on a tarp to the top of a small hill, where we sat quietly while Dave dug a grave for him, grief stricken.

Our German shepherd, Kai, was buried in our backyard. Many of the dearly beloved dead were buried where they shouldn't have been.

County law dictated that we should call a company called Bausback. They picked up dead animals for free, and were paid by the state. Bausback had a fleet of big yellow trucks that were as heavy and rounded as trucks made by Tonka, and the contrast between their cartoon shape and their mission made them all the more sinister. As with garbage trucks, the bed was covered and had a door that opened to reveal the machinery where the animals were transported.

Every time I saw a Bausback truck in town I couldn't help following it. This was a good way to keep up with animal gossip, and also to see some of the more shocking aspects of nature. I had seen cats, dogs, birds, and rabbits slung into the Bausback maw, and once a whole goat, which really surprised me, because I didn't know of anything that could kill a goat.

I was riding around in the cemetery at the edge of town when I saw the Bausback truck go by that Saturday afternoon. I was waiting for Julie to get off duty pumping gas and join me, but I didn't stick around and wait for her. I took off after the truck, my legs pumping and the streamers at the end of my handlebars flying out behind me like circus-colored hair.

I was still a block from Ruth Huff's when the smell hit me, which was the usual smell of her house multiplied many, many times. The whole volunteer fire department was gathered outside, plus Astor Main's scary hearse, the Bausback truck, and sixteen assorted townspeople, including my dad, who met me halfway to the commotion.

"Zip, you just turn around and head home. This is no place for you."

"Nuhn uhn, there's no way I'm going home," I said, scrambling off my bike and heading for the conflagration.

"Now wait a minute," he said, grabbing me by the arm. "Since when did *you* start telling *me* what you're going to do?" He was serious. He was all bent down in my face with his big eyes and smoky breath.

"Since just this one time. If you're going to whup me, go ahead, because I'm planning on staying right here."

He let go of my arm.

"Okay?"

He crossed his arms over his chest and looked down at me like a big Injun. He was thinking of the kind of what-for he was going to give me.

"I'm going to say this one time: are you listening?" His voice was so deep it made my chest rattle. I nodded.

"I'm going to let you stay down here but you have to hold my hand, and if you turn out like your sister I'm going to turn you upside down and spit in your butt, are we clear?" I nodded again, without cracking a smile. He'd been making the same threat my whole life.

The fact that Ruth Huff was dead was of no great concern to most; we had seen it coming for a while. People weren't even especially titillated by the fact that it appeared that some of the cats had been snacking on her in the four or five days she lay undiscovered (although this bothered me immeasurably, since I thought I had seen just about all of nature there was to see, and this was truly new). The reason that so many people were gathered across the street from the dead woman's house, and the reason that two more Bausback trucks had been called, was because some number of expired animals had been found in Ruth's basement—not buried, just thrown down there.

I stood across the street holding Dad's hand as the Bausback men (whom I hoped would someday be sent treasures straight from God) began bringing up the corpses, one at a time, and throwing them into the waiting trucks. I finally had to tie Dad's hanky around my face to keep from fainting, and I noticed that in addition to smoking extra fast, Dad kept sticking his Vicks Inhaler up his nose.

They brought up dogs and cats, some that barely retained their original shape, some that I had seen alive only a few days before. I counted them as they were tossed in the truck: twenty, thirty, forty, fifty. Sixty-seven. There were sixty-seven dead animals in that dark house. She lived with them. She never told anyone and she never asked for any help. Then I realized what I had unconsciously been waiting for, and pulled away from Dad, heading for the Bausback men.

"Where—" Dad started, trying to catch my arm.

"They haven't brought out King, Dad, what if he's alive in there, I just think someone ought to check," I said, stumbling forward.

"Sweetie, stop. Stop. I mean it—turn around." His voice wasn't louder, it was softer, which was twice as bad. "They'll find him," he said. I put my head in his stomach and he patted my trembling back. "They'll find him."

King had been in bed with her, and they brought him out last. Sixty-eight.

———

UNFORTUNATELY FOR ME, Edythe lived on and on, through some unholy pact made with the universe. Every morning at seven she left her house and marched to the post office, where she saluted the flag and whistled "The Star-Spangled Banner." Once a year she took down her gruesome hair and washed it, then sat out in her yard in a straight-back chair, swinging her hair from side to side, a process my dad called Blowing The Stink Off. Her whiskers got longer, then turned white. She never stopped hating me.

One afternoon, as Dad and I dawdled in the porch swing, I saw PeeDink hunting in Edythe's yard.

"That cat doesn't have a lick of sense," I said, sighing.

"Well, honey, he's not right in the head," Dad said, flipping his cigarette into the front yard.

I glared at him. "And just what do you mean by that?"

Dad counted on his fingers. "He's cross-eyed; he jumps out of trees after birds and then doesn't land on his feet; he sleeps with his head smashed up against the wall, and the tip of his tail is crooked."

"Oh, yeah? Well, how about this: he once got locked in a basement by evil Petey Scroggs in the middle of January and survived on snow and little frozen mice. When I'm cold at night he sleeps right on my face. Of that whole litter of kittens he came out of he's the only one left. One of his brothers *didn't even have a butthole.*"

"I stand corrected. PeeDink is a survivor."

While we were talking PeeDink had climbed up a pine tree next to Edythe's house and was walking around on her roof. We watched helplessly as he jumped on her chimney and looked curiously inside, then took one step too many and went straight down. Vanished.

"Ooh, I can't watch," I said, pulling my knees up in front of my eyes.

"On the count of three—ready? One. Two. And three!"

And PeeDink came sailing out of Edythe's front door. He did a little somersault, then stood up and shook himself off, as he had the last six times he had fallen down her chimney. He was sooty and a little crooked, but my cat, and alive, all the same.

Dad stood up. "I'll go get a towel."

As I was wiping him off PeeDink made his crazy, rumbly purr and looked at me lovingly with his crossed eyes. "She just doesn't know what a good stew you would make, does she, punkin'?" I whispered to him, and what I felt toward Edythe was grateful.

"Daddy, can I ask you something?"

"Shoot," he said, flicking the lid of his lighter open and closed, nervously.

"Do you love Lindy more, you know, because she's your real daughter?" It pained me to say it, but I had to know.

"Aw, honey," he said, scratching the back of his head and generally looking miserable. "I guess we should have told you before now."

"What?! What?!"

"Melinda isn't really my daughter. Slim Jenkins is actually her dad." He said it as if he'd found his peace a long time ago.

"Slim Jenkins?! That old drunk? The garbageman?! Daddy, he sleeps in a shed with a bunch of coon dogs! He can't be her father! He smells like a dead possum!"

"Well, this is probably something you should take up with your mother, Zip. After all, it's really her story." And he walked off into the backyard to inspect the fledgling peach tree he was trying to save, mysteriously, with Mother's pantyhose.

I lay down in a worm hole and looked at the sky. I had plenty to think about. A bob-white was calling from the meadow behind the Mooreland Friends Church. A chigger nestled into my leg. It would be another warm night.

PROFESSIONALS

Icouldn't always go to Julie's farm, and so I also had a best friend in town called Rose. There were a number of benefits to Julie's silence, and one of them was that we never exchanged a cross word. Rose, though. She spoke her own mind, *and* she didn't want to be a farmer or ride in a rodeo. Rose was going to be an artist. She was left-handed, which was very rare in Mooreland. She was also a Catholic; her family were the only Catholics in town. I believe it is safe to say that she was surely the only left-handed Catholic any of us had ever seen, so it made sense she would be artistic.

Her specialty was a long, skinny flower with a stem that curved in a left-handed way. It was unusual. She decided to branch out into portraits, and asked me to sit for her. We were in her bedroom in chairs that faced each other. They were excellent strong chairs: just that week Rose and her younger sister Maggie had hung upside down from them, as Bob and Betty Bat, as I, Preacher Bat, had joined them in holy matrimony. When it was time for them to kiss I had to quick slip a piece of paper between their mouths.

I sat very still. Rose looked up at me, then down at her sketch pad, where she made little scritchy sounds. She looked up at me again; down; scritch. I realized I had absolutely no idea what my face was doing. I could have been drooling for all I knew. The room was completely silent except for Rose's pencil, as if we were wrapped in gauze. I could no longer control my face because something amazing was happening to my body. It started with a kind of tickle at the back of my neck which spread like heat to my limbs. I was so thoroughly relaxed I might have actually been asleep, except my mind was perfectly clear. This whole thing, the process of being drawn, was so pleasurable it had to be wrong.

After that first day I wanted Rose to draw me all the time. I didn't care about the portraits—they were all kind of left-handed. I sat for her a few more times, and then one afternoon she announced she had decided to collect boxes instead. I asked her how many boxes she had and she said four. She had the little white box Tone soap came in, a box that had held a tube of lipstick, a smallish but entirely standard cardboard box, and her prize, a very small, square jewelry box her mother had brought home from Acapulco. Her parents were very worldly, and here was the evidence: the box was not only lined with red velvet, the outside was entirely covered with little shells. They poked up a bit sharply, which some might consider a design flaw, but the overall effect was captivating. I tried to figure out how to steal it. I tried to effect a trade—I told her about all the fabulous boxes *just lying around* at my house—but she said she couldn't trade it because it was a souvenir. I told her if she was a real friend she'd trade it. She said if I was a real friend I wouldn't ask, which made me *spitting* mad, so I had to go home.

As I was walking down the stairs I turned back and looked at her sadly. "And I thought you were an *artist*."

At that time Maggie also knew what she wanted to be when she grew up. She was going to be a disc jockey, and toward that end she spent many hours saying, "Solid Gold. WLBC, 104 FM. Solid Gold. WLBC, 104 FM. Solid Gold. WLBC, 104 FM." She was very convincing, and I found myself in awe of her prematurely deep voice.

One afternoon I took my little blue tape recorder with me to their house. My dad had gotten it for my sister, who competed in speech contests, so she could record her speeches and listen to them later. I had quietly and extra sneakily made it my own. Besides my bicycle and PeeDink, there was nothing in the world I loved more. It had only one knob, which you moved around like a gearshift (left to rewind, right for fast forward, up to play, down to record), and a detachable microphone. Hiding behind the couch in the den I had recorded whole conversations between my parents, without them ever knowing. I had yet to discover all of its uses.

"Now look, Maggie. Just say your piece right here into this little microphone and I'll tape it, then you can hear what you sound like."

Maggie wasn't the least bit shy. She tried it with the microphone far away, and with the microphone right up against her mouth. She must have said Solid Gold for ten solid minutes. When I played it back for her she looked absolutely pleased. Recording only confirmed her vocation for her. We both felt so festive that we invited Rose to join us in singing "The Lion Sleeps Tonight" into the microphone. We were all great singers.

I SPENT A LOT OF TIME trying to figure out what I was going to be when I grew up. There were just so many things I was good at. For instance, I could run across the living room and dive into a headstand on the couch, with my legs slapping the wall behind it. Sometimes I would make my parents sit and watch me do this fifteen times in a row.

"Ladies and Gentlemen, it's another perfect ten for Zippy!" Dad would shout, while my mother clapped politely. I tended to do it until my neck got twisted, which would make me *incredibly* mad. Sometimes I had to stomp out of the house saying I hated that sport and would never do it again.

I was also very good at Interview. What follows is an actual transcript from a tape I made with my mother:

Me: "Mom. Mom. Mom. Hey. Let's do Interview."

Mom: "Not now, sweetheart. Let me just finish this arm." [Note: She was knitting a sweater.]

We hear the "Me" character snort unhappily into the microphone, and then something that sounds remarkably like cat fur. The recorder is shut off abruptly, and then comes back on.

Me: "Hey, Mom. Mom. Mamamamamam. Let's do Interview now."

Mom: "We will. I'm almost done with this."

There is generalized stomping and fury. The recorder is shut off, and then comes back on.

Me: "Jesus loves me, this I know. For the Bible tells me so. Lootle ones to heem belonga. They are weak but he is stronga. Mom. Mom. It is time for Interview?"

Mom: "If you don't stop pestering me I'll never finish this sleeve and then we'll never play Interview."

A little primal throaty sound. The recorder is shut off. Comes back on.

Mom: "Good evening, and welcome to Interview. Let's just go straight to our guest and have her tell us her name. Can you tell us your name, miss?"

Me: "No."

Mom: [surprised] "Don't you know your name?"

Me: "No."

Mom: "Okay, then, is there something else you'd like to tell our audience?"

Me: "Not today."

Mom: "Well, then. I guess we'll just sign off. Would you like to say good-bye?"

Me: "No."

Tape is shut off.

———

I WAS ALSO *SO* GOOD with animals. Once when I was walking to my friend Laurie Lee's house I saw a woodpecker on a telephone pole, exactly level with my face. He seemed to be pecking in slow motion. I stepped up to watch him. He pecked! then slooowwwly pulled his beak back. Then peck! then sloooowwwly pulled his beak back. Then peck.

I wrapped my hands around his body. He was stuck in the telephone pole by his beak, so I pulled him out and carried him home, saying calming words over him. I found a shoe box and a baby blanket and wrapped him so that just his little fuzzy red head was sticking out the top. He looked *very* sweet. I left him on the front porch and went tearing in the house, yelling for my mom.

"Mom!! Come quick! There's a sick woodpecker on the porch! I'm keeping it warm!"

Mom came out of her bedroom, where she had recently spent a great deal of time digging through her closet. None of us knew what she was looking for, but it seemed ominous. Periodically, though, she'd come up with a gem, like a stash of Avon lipsticks no bigger than the tip of my finger that she'd found in an old purse. They were the smallest lipsticks ever, and had the names of their colors printed in tiny red letters on the bottoms of the white tubes: Night on the Town, Coral Reef, Strawberry Frost.

"Is it alive?" Mom asked, carrying a pair of blue polyester pants I was praying she wasn't going to cut up into a "jumper" for me.

"Don't know. Can't tell. It ain't moving."

"Don't say ain't. Well, cover it up till your dad comes home."

So I sat on the porch swing with my woodpecker for what must have been a long time. The woodpecker's black eye was all looking at the side of the box. When Dad pulled up to the house in his truck he hit the big hole in front of the tree that had water in it year-round, splashing the water onto the tree and the sidewalk, like he did every day. He got out of the truck, flipped his cigarette toward Edythe's house, and hitched up his pants, like he did every day. He noticed me sitting on the swing with the shoe box.

"Gotcha a dead bird there, Zip?"

"Yep. It's a woodpecker. Got stuck in a telephone pole. I rescued it."

"Good for you. Let's take a look."

I delicately turned back the receiving blanket to reveal the whole of the woodpecker's body, including its yellow feet, which were more decidedly scrunched up than the last time I looked.

"Oh, yeah," Dad said, looking the bird up and down. "You've got a dead woodpecker, all right. Want to bury it?"

"Hmmm. I don't know. I was thinking I might keep it for a while, maybe see if I can get it better."

"I don't think there's gonna be much getting better for this bird. He's got it as good as it gets. Look: he's got a soft blanket and his own box. Let's go ahead and just put him in the ground with the others before all these cats get wind of him."

So we buried him in the garden. I was also very good at digging holes.

NOW THERE WAS SIMPLY no one more professional at strays than my sister. She was a one-woman Humane Society when it came to sick or wounded animals; our house was virtually saturated with them. But she also took in people, which wouldn't have occurred to me. She must have noticed that it wouldn't have occurred to me—I can't imagine any other reason why she wanted me to accompany her to the Kizer encampment, and so close to Halloween.

Tom Kizer took in foster children by the dozen. He had built five or six little houses on a pretty big lot on Jefferson Street, and the kids were scattered through them by age and gender. The townspeople suspected that he was making a fair profit on the children, who were packed together and ill treated, but no one ever confronted him.

I had never been inside any of the little houses, which were all the same—white with blue trim. Melinda was baby-sitting me that evening, and said she had something to take care of with Mr. Kizer. The night was cold and clear and as we walked our breath steamed out in ribbons.

"Lindy. Hey. Whatcha got to talk to Mr. Kizer about?"

"He wants me to help take care of some of his kids. I'm going to see if we can agree on what he pays me."

"He's gonna *pay* you?" I asked, disbelieving. The idea that she might get paid for baby-sitting cast my sister in a whole new light.

"Don't just stop in the middle of the street like that. Keep up with me. Yes, he's going to pay me."

"Wow. Wow. Do Mom and Dad pay you?"

She just snorted and sped up.

Mr. Kizer himself lived in the first of the houses, the one closest to the street. It was guarded by a mangy foster dog that growled even while Melinda was scratching it behind the ears. As we knocked on the door we could hear all kinds of ruckus going on in the house.

"Sounds like wild Injuns," I whispered to my sister, who hushed me with a look.

Mr. Kizer himself answered the door. He was wearing blue work pants, a white T-shirt, and a brown cardigan. He was in his sock feet. Something about the way he was dressed struck me as askew, but I couldn't say what. Behind him was a whole mess of children, some standing still and sucking on their hair, some jumping around and yelling. The house was strangely dark. There could have been kids in the corners I couldn't even see. I suddenly realized there *was* a kid in a corner, but the fact of her completely stumped me.

My sister had been talking to Mr. Kizer while I surveyed the scene, but I hadn't paid any attention to what they were saying.

"Lindy. Hey." I pulled on her sleeve.

"Excuse me, Tom, just a second." She put her face down next to mine. "What?" she asked, with a sharp little point.

"What's wrong with that girl in the corner?" I whispered, pointing at her.

"I'll tell you on the way home," Melinda answered, smacking my hand down. "Don't point."

The girl was in what I took to be a wheelchair, though I'd never actually seen one, and the whole left side of her body was pulled up tight. Her hands hovered uselessly up near her face and she was drooling, as if she had spent too long being drawn by someone.

"Lindy. Hey. Hey. Lindy."

"Excuse me again, Tom." I could feel my sister's mouth right next to my ear, but I couldn't pull my eyes away from the girl in the corner. "Stop it right now, I mean it. I'll talk to you about it on the way home."

"Lindy," I whispered, "what's wrong with that girl?"

As she straightened back up Melinda casually pulled me closer to her, so that she basically had her arm around my throat. My sister could give it to me and give it to me *hard*, it isn't as if I didn't know that.

"Lindy, hey. Lindy. Melinda. Would you just please tell me what is wrong with that girl?!" I was trying to whisper, but I was exasperated.

She tightened her grip around my throat and kind of lifted me off the floor. "Tom, we have to be going. I'll see you on Wednesday night and we'll work this out."

In seconds we were out the door and on the sidewalk. My feet had never touched the ground. Melinda had me by the arm and she was *dangerously* mad.

"You are so *rude*! I've never in all my life . . . I don't even want to talk to you! You don't even care how you make other people feel. You nearly embarrassed me to death in there, and I can't imagine how that poor child felt. You just walk behind me. I'm not talking to you."

We walked in silence for a few seconds, but I couldn't stand it anymore.

"Lindy? What was wrong with that girl?"

She turned around lightning quick, grabbing me by the arm and giving me a quick shake. I was a tall child, but only weighed about seven pounds, so when she pulled my left arm east, my right arm, my head, and both my legs went west. By this time we were in front of Roscoe Brown's house. Roscoe had always been favorably disposed toward me, so I hoped he might be out on his porch and would give my sister the what-for. But no Roscoe.

Now she was dragging me and talking through her clenched teeth at the same time. "I can't believe all the ways Mom and Dad have gone wrong with you, it just makes me crazy. You act like you don't even have a heart! This summer you didn't even cry at *Bambi*! What is wrong with you?!"

I was trying to think of how to tell her why I didn't cry at Bambi even though my heart was broken, when we turned the corner at Reed and Mary Ball's house. We were almost home.

"Lindy? What was wrong with that girl?"

Melinda took a deep breath, then let it out in a cold cloud. She reached out for my hand, quick to anger and quick to forgive. "She was just born that way, honey."

It was an answer I hadn't really expected. She was born that way? It was as if Melinda had both answered my question and refused to answer it. She looked down at me, waiting for me to devil her even more. It was a still kind of look, like the moment when a seesaw is perfectly straight. I had appeared in her life almost without warning when she was ten years old, when she thought she knew what her life was about, and who she was. What she became was my sister. She led me off the dark street and into our house, gently, like a pro.

CHANCE

No. No. Take back this card. Give me a different one," I said, shaking my head and thrusting the card at my dad.

He sat perfectly still across the dining room table on which no meals were ever taken. "You're giving me back a card I just dealt you?"

"Yes. That's the six of clubs and I don't want it because it's a boy."

"The six of clubs is a boy?"

"I would like to only have girls in my hand, please."

He continued to study me a moment, considering his best tactic.

"Zip: when I deal you a hand of cards you just take what you're given and then we play the game from there. It's a game of chance."

"Well, that's just stupid. Also I don't want this three of diamonds, because even though diamonds are girls, threes are boys. How many cards am I supposed to have?"

"You're supposed to have eleven, but I've only dealt five so far and you've tried to give back two."

"Then could I please have one two three four five six seven eight cards, please? All girls?"

Dad tapped his very wide, blunt fingertips on the table top, then reached over and picked up a book. He opened it up to a very non-specific-looking page in the middle and read aloud: "Players may not refuse to accept cards on the basis of boys or girls. Players must accept hand dealt by their dads."

"Let me see that," I said, speedy-quick reaching across the table to grab the book.

"Nope. Only adults can look at this rule book. There's an age limit. Also, you can't read."

"Two days ago I read the words french fries and frozen Coke, ask Mom. We were sitting at the counter at Grant's in New Castle and I just looked up at the board and read them."

"Can you spell french fries?" Dad asked in a testing sort of way.

"Nope."

"Could it be that you happen to know you can get french fries and frozen Coke at Grant's, and so you said you could read the words on the board because you knew they were up there somewhere?"

"Could be."

"May I please give you this five of diamonds?"

I shook my head yes.

"Okay. What about a queen of spades?"

That one stopped me. It was a girl all right, but not the kind of girl you'd want to hang on to. I took it anyway.

"I don't think that book you read from has anything to do with cards."

"And why would you say that?"

"Because there's a hoot owl on the front of it."

"Good point. What about the seven of hearts?"

Seven was a boy, but the seven of hearts was a very, very sweet boy. I took it.

"Why aren't you at work?" I asked my dad, studying my cards carefully.

"Why aren't you in school?"

I eventually accepted an ace of diamonds, because all aces were girls, even the ace of spades. The two of clubs came next, which I debated, but accepted. Dad went right past the nine of spades—no way. The other red five I took; another queen (although the queens made me nervous); a lonely four that could have been a boy at another time, and finally, the eight of spades. Eights were completely girls, but the black eights were girls who were maybe a little too good at sports.

Dad then dealt his own hand face down, as if he didn't care a lick what he got. He picked up his cards and studied them in his straight-backed way. His face was as blank as the face of a wild Injun.

"What do I do now?" I asked.

"The object of the game is to put together sets of threes, three cards that match. Do you have three cards that match, like three aces?"

I stared at him.

"No. You don't. Okay, then. What we're going to do is take turns getting cards from this pile right here. You decide on a card you don't want anymore and discard it, then take a new one, and try to put together three sets of three. When you have three sets of three, you put your extra card on the pile when it's your turn and you win the hand."

"Who goes first at discharging?"

"You do, because I dealt to you. You actually have eleven cards, so when you discharge you'll have ten."

"I'd rather not."

He looked at me blankly for a moment. "You'd rather not what?"

"I'd rather not go first."

Some more sitting around saying nothing followed, then Dad carefully studied his hand, and chose one to discard. He placed it on top of the spare cards with a little snap.

"Zippy? What's the name of this game?"

"I can't remember."

"Gin," he said, and spread his cards out on the table. The winning hand was all boys, in sets of three: three kings, three jacks, and three ugly tens, lined up like war veterans in front of the drugstore. He stood up, slid his cigarettes and silver lighter across the table and into his breast pocket, and headed for the door.

"I'll see you later," he said as he stepped out onto the front porch. "Good game."

"Thanks," I called after him. I continued to sit at the table for quite a while, sorting out the girls and putting them in a little girl pile where they'd be safe. For good measure I put all the boys back in the box with the Joker, where they belonged.

A SHORT LIST OF
THINGS MY FATHER
LOST GAMBLING

1. My pony, Tim. He was excellently small
and nice, and lived in the meadow behind the
Mooreland Friends Church, with no one's permission. One day I came home from school,
and poof. If it were not for a photograph I have
of me astride the little horse, with his name and
mine written on the back by my mother, I
would for certain think I'd made him up.

2. A small motorcycle. It appeared on the front porch one morning; no one learned to drive it; shortly thereafter, it was gone.

3. My mother's engagement and wedding rings. The wedding band was heavy gold, with a little cluster of shooting stars that even had tails. In the center of each star was a diamond chip. In my imagination she just looked down one day, and they had vanished.

4. A boat. Like the motorcycle, it simply appeared. We lived nowhere near water, but every day I went out and pretended to drive it at abnormal speeds across choppy waters. For a brief time it took the place of rodeo as my favorite sport.

5. My twenty-five-dollar savings bond. I won it at the Mooreland Fair in a game of intense skill and concentration called Guess How Many Pennies Are in This Huge Jar. I guessed 468 and *got it exactly right*. My name was announced just before the Grand Champion pull at the Horse and Pony Pull, the zenith of the Mooreland social season. Twenty-five dollars was an unheard of amount of money at the time, and my father volunteered to deposit it in my "savings account" for me, which I had never heard of before that moment. Over the next few years I probably asked him for the money 736 times, and he always assured me we were just waiting for it to mature.

6. A wide variety of excellent hunting beagles.

A SHORT LIST OF THINGS
MY FATHER WON GAMBLING

1. A wide variety of excellent hunting beagles.

2. A stuffed monkey, which became my most beloved toy. His arms and legs were red and his torso was white, as if he were wearing a long-sleeved union suit. His face and hands and feet were rubber, and he was holding a partially peeled banana that fit superbly in his mouth. He had a jaunty look on his face, and his feet were molded like little tennis shoes. I can't say enough about how fabulous he was.

3. Guns: rifles, handguns, muzzle loaders, etc. His favorite shotguns he kept on a rack above the couch in the den; in the drawer of the rack was a small glass tube with a rubber stopper in which he kept my baby teeth.

4. A strange friend named Burns. He had two daughters who appeared to me to be stolen from their rightful owners, and a profitable little enterprise called the Holiday Cleaners. The gambling group met in the hidden basement of this business. Burns was eventually found dead, shot through the alleged cranium; he was found in the aforementioned basement. No charges were ever filed. (I should probably also list him in the Lost category.)

5. Money. When he came home with any, regardless of whether our lights were about to be turned off again, we jumped in his truck and went out to dinner, then often to the Dusk to Dawn movies at the Sky-Hi Drive-In. I saw all of the Planet of the Apes movies this way, back to back. It was heaven.

THE WORLD
OF IDEAS

My grandmother Mildred, who adopted my mom when she was a baby, called our house one Sunday afternoon. Mom answered.

"Hello?"

"Dee Dee?" Mildred's voice could sharpen pencils. "Where are you?"

"Mother, where did you call?"

"How come you're not in church?"

Dad could hear Mildred's voice eking out

the edges of the receiver, which caused him to grimace involuntarily.

"Church got out a little while ago. Now I'm home."

"I've got a question for you. Mabel Simpkins told me today that the Jesus who died at Easter was the same one who was born at Christmas. Is that true?" Mildred was a proper medium-well Methodist, as befitted her standing as a moneyed old woman in a small, depressed city. Dad used to say that half the population of New Castle, Indiana, came in on the back of a flatbed truck from Kentucky, all related.

Before Mom could answer, Mildred continued. "I just laughed at Mabel and told her she sure wasn't making a fool of me. I know Easter comes before Christmas."

Mom closed her eyes, as if in prayer. Her expression was that of a person being poked with a straight pin, but enduring it, stoically.

"We don't choose our relatives," she always said.

"Damn shame," was my dad's reply.

MY MOM WAS A PERSON who had some ideas, and she'd been having them for a long time. For instance, her birth mother left only one request at the orphanage where she dropped off my mom, when she was nine months old: that she be raised Catholic. Her new parents gave it an honest shot, but Mom consistently got in bad trouble during catechism for asking questions. She couldn't stop herself. Finally, when she was ten years old, the nuns were discussing the candles that signified the presence of God in the church, and before Mom could stop herself her hand shot in the air and the sister called her name, *Delonda?* rather despondently, and my mom asked if the candles went out did God leave? And that was it. They asked *her* to leave. My mother is the only person I've ever met who was excommunicated before puberty.

Then she got to junior high and she and one of her best friends, Marjorie, got in an argument and Marjorie got permanently mad at her, which caused Mom no end of heartache, since everyone else flat-out loved her. Mom was extremely popular, by design. Realizing at a young age (with assistance from Mildred, who often told her she was ugly) that she would not be petite or blond or conventionally pretty, she set out to be the funniest and kindest person in her school, a friend to everyone, and she succeeded. That she could alienate a friend she truly loved was a grievous thing, and in her desperation she went to Marjorie's house and when Marjorie asked what she wanted Mom said, "I just wanted to tell you I'm dying of a brain tumor." Marjorie immediately put aside the slight, and then proceeded to tell everyone else in the school, and everyone became astronomically fond of Mother for a long time, in preparation for the grief of losing her. Later she was cured by a miracle, and it was a terrific relief to her many, many friends.

THE FIRST TIME I ever truly grasped the concept of chromosomes, and the transmission of DNA, I was sitting in the truck with Dad, giving him some sideways looks. Earlier that day I had walked into a bait shop, and before I could say anything, the old man behind the counter had said, "You must be Bob Jarvis's daughter." I was unaccustomed to looking in mirrors, with good reason, but after that comment, all the way to the lake, I peeked into the big side mirror on Dad's truck, trying to see what the old man saw. I looked at myself. I looked at my dad. My suspicion that I hadn't actually been purchased from gypsies, as my family insisted, seemed to be confirmed.

It appeared that I had been split down the middle by my parents, genetically, to my misfortune. I had my dad's curly hair and his long face and his very big, round eyes, but my eyes were close set, like my mom's. I had Mom's nose and her little square chin and her tiny mouth, with Dad's huge teeth in them. I had Dad's giraffe neck and his hands and feet and Mom's short torso and long legs. On the whole, I couldn't imagine a worse outcome. I slumped against the truck door.

There was a great deal I didn't understand about chromosomes, to be perfectly honest. I'd need to go to Rose's and ask her. I started thinking about what it meant that I had Dad's eyes, and I came to this conclusion: if I inherited what made his eyes his, wouldn't it follow that I also inherited what his eyes had seen—what they knew? And if I had his hands, wouldn't my hands know how to do some things that he taught them a long time ago, skills his hands had learned from those that came before his? It was an idea that made me bigger than I had been and smaller than I might be later: my mother was good at reading books (reading them out loud, too), making cinnamon biscuits, and coloring in a coloring book. Also she was a good eater of popcorn and knitter of sweaters with my initials right in them. She could sit really still. She knew how to believe in God and sing really loudly. When she sneezed our whole house rocked. My father was a great smoker and driver of vehicles. Also he could whistle like a bird and could perform any task with either his left or right hand, a condition he taught me was called "ambisexual." (When I told my teacher about this skill, she quick put her hand over my mouth and told me some things were best kept in the family.) He could hold a full coffee cup while driving and never spill a drop, even going over bumps. He lost his temper faster than anyone.

Looked at this way, it appeared that the rest of my life would be remarkably like the present, only I would get bigger and have to take up smoking.

MILDRED LIVED IN THE FIRST-FLOOR apartment of a beautiful old house in New Castle. The house had a driveway that started at the street and went up a hill right into the middle of the side yard, missing her garage by a good fifteen feet. It was a puzzle. I always assumed it was a design flaw, or a whim, but my mom finally told me it was the result of a tornado that had picked the whole house up and moved it over twenty or so feet, plopping it down directly over the family graveyard. And she was right; standing on Mildred's front porch you could see half a dozen old tombstones flattened and sticking out from under the foundation of the house like the legs of the Wicked Witch. One of the tombstones had been leveled face up, so that the words were legible. It had marked the grave of a boy named Daniel, who died young of unnamed causes. I asked my mom if that was where she had gotten my brother's name and she said, gracious, I hope not.

Inside, Mildred's house was beautiful and genteel, without a false note. A spotless white carpet covered the hardwood floors. The antiques were expensive pieces in pristine condition; on her marble-faced fireplace was a clock that never lost time and a bust of Apollo that Mildred called Clark Gable. Mom once tried to tell her who Apollo was, but Mildred just waved her hands, irritated. She would have no part of explanations.

I was especially taken with the bathroom. The tin ceiling was unusually high, and the walls were covered with pink tile. The floor was tile, too, so that the whole room felt cold and echoey. It looked pink, but it didn't feel pink. Some of the tiles had designs which, upon closer inspection, were revealed to be flamingoes. The man who lived in the apartment before my grandmother had been a bachelor doctor, and he had hung himself in this very bathroom, from a large hook that had been designed to hold a fern. The hook was still there.

I watched Mildred carefully for signs that she might be affected, which is not to say haunted, by the fact that her house 1) had been moved twenty feet by a tornado; 2) was sitting on top of a graveyard; 3) bore the mark of a terrible death scene. When I mentioned it to her she simply said pshaw and went on about her business, which was usually cleaning. She was the only person I ever knew who dusted her lightbulbs.

Mildred's idea of a joke was a cup that had printed on the side YOU SAID HALF A CUP! It was a cup cut in half. Her idea of dessert was large-pearl tapioca, a culinary item that appears to be on the endangered list. Biting into those pearls, which were approximately the size of adult peas, provided the same little thrill of a soft giving-way and then a crunch that one ordinarily only got from the cartilage in a chicken breast. I loved it, and ate every pearl separately, which drove Mildred to distraction.

"You'd better eat that faster," she'd shriek at me after lunch.

"No, thank you," I'd say, concentrating on catching an especially juicy one.

"That's just ridiculous, what you're doing."

"I like it this way." Her spindly and antique dining room chairs were tall, and perfect for swinging one's feet as one ate.

"Hmmmph," she'd say, picking up her silver cigarette case and her lighter. "Stop swinging your legs."

Mildred smoked, beautifully, for sixty-five years. Shortly after she turned eighty she called my mom and said she had heard at church that smoking was bad for her health. Was that true? Mom affirmed that it was. Mildred put her cigarettes down and never picked them up again. She claimed they never crossed her mind, a sentence that caused Dad merely to raise his eyebrows.

I WENT TO ROSE's HOUSE to talk to her about science, and inheritance. I was wearing my old saddle oxfords and, as an experiment, a dress that I had picked up at a rummage sale. It was a few sizes too big, which kept me from feeling it much. Over the top of the dress I was wearing a raincoat Mom Mary had passed along, which was pink and gray and black plaid. I'd never seen an uglier thing. The combination of dress and raincoat made me feel like a new person, a serious and curious person, and I was anxious to show myself off to Rose.

She couldn't come outside right away, because she and Maggie were cleaning. They did a lot of the cleaning in their house, which I considered to be a sign of immoral parenting. The job of parents, as I saw it, was to watch television and step into a child's life only when absolutely necessary, like in the event of a tornado or a potential kidnapping.

Rose said I could wait outside for her, on the swing set. I swung across the monkey bars for a while, then climbed up on top of them. I decided to jump down from there, because I'd never done it before. I landed so hard that my ankles stung, and my heels felt like they'd been pushed up into the back of my leg. I climbed up and did it again, then finally Rose popped her head out the back door and said if I didn't stop pretty soon she might see my panties, which was a dress-wearing dilemma I hadn't considered. She suggested that maybe I could just swing for a few minutes, so I sat down on the swing and looked out over her neighbors' yard and thought.

I wonder how long it's going to take Rose to get out here, was my first thought, and then, *I wonder how long I've already been waiting. I've already been out here a long time, and my mom says you can never relive a single moment.* I stopped swinging. A single moment. Individual blades of grass became very distinct in my vision, as they sometimes do in the light of thickly clouded days. *I am thinking of a moment—it is gone. Here's another—gone. Gone. Gone.* One cannot consider, with any real accuracy, the currency of a single moment and its extinction. Those are not the words I thought, but I felt them. The ground spun beneath me, although I was sitting still. I stood up too fast and became light-headed and had to grab ahold of the swing set's ladder, which was striped like a barber's pole, I noticed for the first time. I wandered out of Rose's yard and headed home as if I were sick. It was impossible to stop thinking about time; I couldn't get it out of my head and the effect was that every step I took was measured in jerky increments that vividly illustrated the arrival of a little unit of time and the death of that unit, until I was nauseous.

The old brass doorknob on our front door was colder and more familiar than anything I'd ever touched. It seemed that my hand was connected to it for a long time, longer than necessary, and then I was inside and the house was dark and nearly humid with the lack of industry inside it. It smelled exactly like the only thing in the world I knew for sure. A lamp burned on the table beside my mother's end of the couch, and I found her sitting there reading, the television on with the sound low but insistent.

I unbelted Mom Mary's raincoat and sat down on the couch beside my mother. She asked if I was feeling all right.

"Have you ever thought about something too hard and gotten dizzy?" I asked her.

I could see by the look on her face that she probably, in fact, spent most of her life dizzy. She said, "Do you know anything about astronomy?"

"Yes. I'm a Pisces."

"That's astrology. Do you know anything about the stars?"

I shook my head.

"Well, when I was about your age, I learned about the stars and galaxies and planets for the first time. It was all just an idea to me at first, while I was still at school. Then one night I went out into the yard—this was while my daddy was still alive, and we lived in Whiting—and looked up at the stars like I had many times before, but this time I saw them in the context of the *size* of space, and our place in it. I saw that the universe was vast and unknowable, and that we were just tiny little specks that vanished before anything had even taken note of us being here. And you know what happened when I realized that?"

"What?" I said, kind of whispering.

"I fell straight down on the ground."

"You didn't."

"I just fell right down on my back, as if I'd fainted, only I was still aware of everything around me, including what had made me fall down in the first place, which made me think I might never be able to get up again."

"So what happened?"

"My dress started getting wet from dew, which was uncomfortable enough that I stopped thinking about the stars and went inside and my dad gave me a drink of beer."

"Wow."

"My dad believed in beer."

I sat for a few minutes looking at the floor. I still didn't feel so good.

"Do you want to tell me what you were thinking about?" She laid her hand on my back.

"Nothing. It doesn't matter."

We continued sitting there a while, then I got up and headed for the door. If I hurried, I might make it to Rose's before the rain began.

"Sweetheart?" Mom called as I started through the curtain that separated the den from the living room. I looked back at her.

"You'll be all right. You're going to be fine."

I nodded. Once on the porch I decided I could get everywhere faster if I jumped, so I leaped down the stairs and hopped like a frog down to the corner, and from there I just took off running.

LOCATION

Dana entered my life like a firestorm in the middle of our second-grade year. On that fateful day I was dropping all the items out of my desk one by one, trying to get Sammy Bellings to bend over and pick them up, because she had once again come to school in a dress too small for her, without any panties.

Sammy sat next to me, and Roger sat on the other side. I didn't even pretend to like him, the way the nice children did. He always smelled like he had peed in his pants, and he had epilepsy. He was skinny, and he had little gray monkey fingers that gave me the hookey-spooks. They were the fingers of a career nose picker. Once he had fallen right out of his desk while having a small seizure, and all I could do was watch, frozen with shock and fear. I hated medical emergencies. I was convinced that sick people were dangerous, like wounded animals, a misconception that was compounded when, during Roger's seizure, our first-grade teacher yelled, "Stay away from his mouth! Don't put your hands in his mouth!" My horror was only increased when I asked my dad what on earth might compel a person to put her hand in the mouth of a seizing person, and he said, I swear, *to grab his tongue, so he couldn't swallow it.*

I was down to one last crayon, and I was about to drop it in front of Sammy when Mrs. Caroline, our plump and very kind teacher, answered a knock at the classroom door. It was the principal, Mr. Moore, and he had his hands on the shoulders of a . . . well, the shoulders of Dana. The two of them escorted Dana in and stood her in front of the class, and when I got a good look at her I dropped the crayon by accident, which caused Sammy to bend over and pick it up, which in turn caused the class to collapse with laughter for the eleventh time that day. Mrs. Caroline gave me her soft and long-suffering look. I was killing her. Mr. Moore cleared his throat principally, unaware that we were laughing at Sammy's smiling brown bottom and not at Dana, whose general demeanor did not invite ridicule.

She was not as tall as I was. But she was very wiry, and her skin was dark, and I couldn't tell if it was a tan or if she was just born that way. Her hands were strong and masculine looking, with blunt, clean fingernails, like my father's, and the back of her hands were ropy with thick blue veins. I'd never seen that on a girl before. She had a long, brown neck, and her hair was also long and brown and aggressively straight, and her eyes were brown and slanted up in the corners. Unlike nearly everyone else in our class, she had all of her permanent teeth, and they weren't clunky and square and oversized, but long, white, and adult. Dana's face was completely finished. By the time she was seven years old, she had grown into the face she would have all the rest of her life.

Now all of this was problematic and titillating, but not unbearable. The one detail that none of us could overcome or tear our eyes away from was her miniature, black leather biker jacket, with five zippers. Motorcycles themselves were just a rumor in Mooreland in 1972, but hoodlum dress was out of the question. In addition to the jacket, Dana wore scuffy little Levi's, and black boots. They were not cowboy boots. She caught me staring at her and tilted her chin up in a defiant and challenging way.

"Children," Mrs. Caroline began, "I'd like you to welcome our new student, Dana. She has just moved here from Los Angeles, California. Can anyone here show us on the map where we would find California?"

Los Angeles, California. I let a little whistle escape through my teeth, the way my sister had taught me. When it became clear that no one in the room knew how to find L.A., Dana walked over herself and pointed to it on the map.

"This is it, right here," she said, as confidently as if she were the teacher. She pointed to a large area way over at one edge of the map, and down low.

"Very good, Dana. Is there anything you'd like to tell us about where you came from?" Mrs. Caroline often sounded bored, or drugged, but I guessed she was just exhausted.

"Sure," Dana said, shrugging her shoulders. "There are more people in the city of Los Angeles than in the whole state of Indiana. We have palm trees and the sun shines all year long and there is no winter and all the famous movie stars in the world live there."

I looked over at Julie and made a little nyah-nyah-nyah face. I desperately needed moral support. Julie looked as stunned as the rest of us.

Mrs. Caroline exchanged a tired glance with Mr. Moore, and sighed. "Thank you, Dana. You seem to know a lot about California. Why don't you just take that empty desk right there," and she put Dana right in front of me.

Sammy Bellings's bottom never crossed my mind the rest of that day. In fact, I didn't think about the alphabet, or coloring my dancing bear page, or how on earth I was going to fit my name between the two solid lines and one dotted line that were supplied to me. As my fat pencil hovered above my Goldenrod pad, I could think about only one thing: that shiny brown hair falling over the collar of the leather jacket in front of me. How my life was over. How nothing would ever, ever be the same.

I FOLLOWED DANA HOME from school. She lived, of course, in the only new house in town. It was built at a slanty modern angle, and rather than being sided with either the traditional painted wood or aluminum, it was covered with stained cedar shingles. The house sat on half an acre, and there was a largish barn in the backyard. It had been sitting empty for almost a year; no one had seen Dana's family move in.

Just as she reached her front porch, Dana wheeled around and yelled, "Are you following me?" Her voice was so deep that it startled me and caused me to jump backward a step. Without looking at her I crossed the street and continued on toward home. In my peripheral vision I could see her standing on her front porch like a traffic cop, with her legs spread and her arms crossed. That leather jacket was so impressive I could smell it and hear it crackling even from a great distance.

THERE WERE IDENTICAL TWINS in my class, Anita and Annette. By any standard, Anita was the sweetest person available, plus she could turn the best cartwheel and bake in an Easy Bake Oven. Annette was quite diverse. She could play any sport and could also draw very handsomely. I sometimes got them as best friends; not together, one at a time, although having one was like having both. I considered them a real best friend coup.

In the third grade, Dana stole them from me. The minute I saw Anita on the teeter-totter with her I knew I was in trouble. I turned to Kirsten, who was a great fall-back best friend, because she had seven brothers and sisters and going to her house was like going to the zoo. Dana stole her from me. I started spending more time with Rose at school, which I didn't like to do because I spent so much other time with her that we hated each other like sisters. Dana stole her, plus she told Rose all the things I had said about her behind her back, like that I thought it was irritating that she was all the time left-handed. That left only Julie in the first tier of best friends, and

Julie could not be monopolized at school. If a good-looking foot-
ball game formed in an afternoon recess, no way would Julie spend
that hour jumping rope with me. Julie had extensive playground
duties, most of which revolved around defending her champi-
onships in every single sport. The afternoon I walked out and saw
Julie and Dana playing H-O-R-S-E, I knew something had to give.

"Hey, Julie," I said, giving her a little wave as I walked onto the
cracked asphalt. She gave me a nod in reply then took her shot,
which she sunk from about fifteen feet.

"I don't remember anyone inviting you over," Dana said, as if
she were genuinely perplexed by my presence. Her voice sounded
like she had spent the whole previous evening screaming. Julie
passed her the ball and Dana tucked it under her arm while she
studied me menacingly for a moment. I said nothing. When she finally turned and shot, from too far away and at a difficult angle, the
ball missed the hoop by a good two feet. H.

"Thanks a lot," she said, with no gratitude. "I missed that shot
because of you."

"Well, I'm glad there was a reason," I said, watching Julie slide
over to take her shot from the same impossible place. Julie walked
so smoothly she might have been on skates. She dribbled twice,
then shot without setting up, and hit it.

"Did I mention 'go away'?" Dana asked, cocking her head and
looking like Los Angeles. I could see that the situation was escalat-
ing, which was good, because as far as my best friendships were
concerned, I had hit rock bottom.

"I think it's your shot again," I answered, nodding toward Julie,
who was holding out the basketball, patiently.

As I watched Dana shoot, I thought of what my brother would

have said about her form. She pushed too hard forward, without applying an arc. She didn't wait for the moment to get itself right before she let the ball leave her hand. There was no follow through in her fingers. Her knees barely bent; her thighs were completely stiff. She would have stood a better chance, even with the unlikely shots, if she had centered her shoulders above her hips. She missed. O.

When Dana bounced the ball angrily back to Julie, I took a few moments to study intently the one boxing lesson I had received from my father. Actually, I focused only on the section which I called Putting Your Hands Up In Front Of Your Face To Prevent Fractures. She stomped over to me and stood so close I was able to smell her skin, which radiated something between hot and scorched.

"You bug me," she said, looking me hard in the eye. "You're interrupting our game and Julie is *my* best friend now." I could see that her right hand was itching for some violence.

I tore my eyes away from Dana, leaving myself vulnerable, and looked at Julie, who was heading toward the area that would become the three-point zone. She looked back at me for just a moment, then shot, and hit it.

When I looked back at Dana I saw just a glimmer of alarm pass over her face as she realized the distance she would have to shoot to stay in the game. She had no idea what being best friends with Julie was all about, or how absurd it was to think that she could really come between us. She might as well have announced she was going to steal my spleen.

Dana approached Julie's position with what was left of her swagger. She wisely concluded that the shot called for some consideration, which she granted the distance and the trajectory, then shot her straight-on shot and missed. R.

"Are you even going to say anything?! Are you going to answer me?" she said, voice raised, as she headed toward me.

"Not yet," I said, watching Julie prepare for a lay-up, which she breezed through and hit.

Dana turned in time to see the shot fall, then looked back at me. She issued a sound I'd heard dogs make at each other when they really wanted to fight but also had to finish their dinner. Julie tossed her the ball, and Dana walked back past the free-throw line. She dribbled a couple times while bouncing on the balls of her feet, then took off.

Her shot was a lay-up in name only. Basically the ball just went straight up the backboard to the right of the rim and straight back down again, barely missing Dana, who wasn't sure where to go after shooting. She finally stepped out of bounds and stood there, dejectedly, while Julie decided where to take her final shot. S.

As she often did when we played, Julie picked the easiest spot on the court, right in front of the foul line, to end the game. It was a shot she could have hit while suffering from malaria.

Dana caught the ball under the basket and walked out slowly to the little jewel of a spot. She dribbled a moment, then looked at the basket hopelessly. Her too-hard shot hit the back of the rim and bounced up hard in the air. Julie watched the ball arc up above the basket, then caught it as it came down. E.

"Did you come over here for a reason?" Dana asked as she walked toward me, with a fair piece of resignation.

"Yes. I wanted to know if you'd like to come over and ride bikes with me after school."

She gave me a you-must-be-kidding look, then spit on the court and rubbed it in with the toe of her boot. "You live in that ugly mustard-colored house behind the Marathon?"

"Yeah. Julie's parents own that station," I said, thinking I might provide her with a little Mooreland information.

"I know that," she said, sneering. "I guess I could ride bikes with you for a while. I just have to make sure the house is clean before my mom gets home at nine."

"Nine *at night?*" I asked, disbelieving. I didn't know any church that held services that late on a Tuesday.

"Yes, nine *at night*. That's when she gets done bowling."

"*Bowling?*" I tried, fruitlessly, to imagine a mother in a bowling alley.

"Are you some kinda parrot? Yes. Bowling. She belongs to a league. They all work at Chrysler."

I bit my tongue to prevent myself from saying *a factory?* The recess bell rang, and Dana and I headed for the line that formed under the big gym door, girls on one side, boys on the other. I turned and looked back at Julie, who was completely oblivious to the political coup I had just pulled off. She was moving around the court, taking various shots. Always, just before she shot, she let the ball fall gently back into the cradle of her hand, which nearly touched her shoulder. It was a beautiful moment. It seemed that everywhere Julie went, there appeared a horse.

"Good game," I told Dana, as we approached the school.

"Shut up," she said, barely nudging me with her stiff shoulder.

———

DANA AND I BEGAN talking with a speech impediment that caused my mother to wish us both harm. It involved making all of our s-sounds at the very back of our mouths, with copious amounts of spit.

"Mom," I would say, "I'm heading over to Dana'zsh houzshe."

"Stop talking that way," Mom would answer, through clenched teeth. She almost never got mad, although once when I was five I had come barreling down the steps, stomped straight into the den where she was talking on the telephone, and demanded that she hang up and make me a peanut butter sandwich. She ignored me. When I demanded louder, and with a furiously stomped foot, she reached up without looking at me and slapped me in the face.

"Okay, I'll zshtop," I'd zshay, heading out the door.

"I'm going to return you to the gypsies," she'd yell, returning to her book.

"Zshorry, Mom, but it'zsh too late for me and the gypzshi-ezsh."

"My mom hatezsh it when we talk like zshish," I told Dana, while rolling around on her huge bed. Everything in her room was gray, and it was all very spartan, like she didn't really live there.

"My mom chazshed me with a yardzshtick," Dana answered.

"Did zshe catzshch you?" I asked, interested.

"No. Zshe only barely made it out the front door before zshe zshtarted wheezshing," Dana laughed. Ha ha on the smokers.

I HEARD MOM tell my dad that Dana's parents' life in Mooreland had all the marks of a second chance gone ugly. And while Lou and

Jo associated with no one in Mooreland, preferring the company of the people they worked with in the factory in New Castle, Dana didn't hesitate to tell her friends at school some of the most intimate details of their life, like: they were atheists. This was crazy and unheard of, and I advised Dana to keep it under wraps. Also, her parents had been married and divorced three times, all to each other. Dana's oldest brother had once smoked marijuana. While high he fell asleep and into a dream about the Wizard of Oz. Just as he dozed off he heard the beginning of "Hotel California," and then he was on the Yellow Brick Road, and the dream went on and on and on, and as he started to awaken he guessed he had been asleep and dreaming for about five hours, but in fact, "Hotel California" was just ending. This was another fact I felt it best no one in Mooreland know.

Dana's mother, Jo, was short and whippet thin with dark hair bleached platinum and the skin of a career smoker. She was very tanned. Dana had inherited her deep, gravelly voice from Jo, and her short temper. I never heard Jo speak to Dana kindly, or maternally, or really in any way at all, except to give housekeeping orders, which Dana performed with a fabulous competence. One afternoon we went to her house after school—there was never anyone there—and Dana noticed that there were dishes to do. Two things stood out for me immediately: one was Dawn dishwashing liquid, which I didn't know existed. We had only ever used Ivory in my house, which made Dawn seem hopelessly blue and exotic. The other was that Dana knew, somehow, when the dishes were done, to wipe down the counter around the sink. She even moved the canisters and wiped behind them. I watched her, puzzled. How did she know how to do that? Who had taught her? Even her hands, the way she held the sponge, and the turn of her arm as she reached the corner of the counter, were superior to anything I'd seen in a person my own age.

Dana's father was the kind of man who bragged excessively about breaking the speed limit. He was big in a general way, with a long stride and rather stooped shoulders. Like his wife, he drank heavily and chain-smoked; he carried a whole roadmap of broken capillaries on his face. His eyes were what scared me most: he wore the look men get in their forties when they've given up hope and plan to get even. Everywhere he walked a vague sense of violence prevailed, although I was never certain whom he had hurt or if he was just a living threat. After working all day at the Chrysler, he and Jo spent the evening drinking and bowling. I rarely saw them.

If I had been left to my own devices the way Dana was, I would have eventually succumbed to both pestilence and malnutrition. My only comfort would have been to die in front of the television, watching Cowboy Bob and his sidekick, Sourdough the Singing Biscuit. But Dana and her two older brothers did just fine. In fact, she ate better than I did, and was at school every day in clean clothes (which I never had), with her homework done, and every time I walked into her jaunty, modern house, it was spotless, so clean it echoed. The new furniture was treated against stains; the carpets were vacuumed relentlessly, even though there were no pets in the house and no shoes past the doorways; no books or roller skates or dirty laundry menaced from the stairs. Dana's house could have been cut from a magazine, the kind of home that tells a story, even though no one lives in it.

FROM THAT FIRST DAY I saw her, in the second grade, all the way through our third, fourth, and fifth grades, these were the things that Dana did better than I: math, science, spelling, reading, history, all things domestic and, once she got over her initial basketball hump, all things sports related. I was disliked by all of my teachers for reasons that were completely mysterious to me, but even in that dubious category, Dana excelled. She was disliked more passionately, sometimes even inciting our teachers to violence, which I had yet to do. For instance, our third-grade teacher, driven to a rage by Dana's wisecracking, shook her until she saw stars. That evening Dana went home and searched through the thousands of magazines her brothers collected until she found an article about the dangerous effects of shaking children, which she cut out. The next morning, while Mrs. Holiday was taking attendance, Dana marched right up and handed it to her. The whole class watched with a nervous excitement, but Mrs. Holiday, who could not be coerced into increasing her own knowledge, simply threw it in the trashcan without reading it.

When we were all invited to a party at Julie's house in the fall of our fourth-grade year, I assumed that my naturally superior relationship with animals and farm implements would be revealed, and in the ledger in which our talents were recorded, I would finally have one little tick in my column. I no longer hoped to beat Dana at anything. I just wanted to be able to say that once, in the wretched life that followed her arrival, I had proved good at something.

The party's beginnings were not auspicious. The Newmans' pole barn was filled with shelled corn, an overwhelming mountain of it, and someone, probably Julie's brother David Lee, who wished us all dead, suggested that we climb up in the rafters of the barn and dive into it.

"What a ridiculous idea," I laughed. "We could suffocate that way—diving into corn is not so different from diving into water, except that it's harder to get out of cor—" Before I could finish the sentence, the rest of the party was out the door and flying toward their doom.

When I reached the barn Julie and Dana had already scampered up the ladder and were making their way across the rafters like cats. When they were directly above the peak of the corn mountain they held hands and dove in. Julie's red hair flew up behind her like a cape; Dana's face was completely transformed by the surprise and joy of her brief free fall. When they hit the corn, surely harder than they had anticipated, they both disappeared for just a moment, then came up spitting, the air around them opaque with dust.

The game continued until everyone had jumped from the rafters; that is, everyone but me, because I was convinced that my father had a special and very limited form of ESP that allowed him to zero in on any situation in which I might be endangering my life. Each time I started to go up the ladder, I had a vision of Dad's truck flying mercilessly into the barn lot. He would be out of the truck and in the barn before I could even begin sputtering excuses, and it was hard to choose which was more humiliating: not jumping, or not jumping and being escorted home by the seat of my pants by a man wearing a firearm. In the end I simply didn't jump, choosing one fate over the other. Julie seemed not to notice, but Dana turned to me with the ironic smile that bespoke her earlier life in A City. She noticed.

We went out to visit three of Julie's horses, Rebel, Diablo, and Mingo. Mingo was Julie's favorite of all the horses, even though he was criminally insane. No one but Julie, not even Big Dave, could ride him, and once while she was on him he had become frightened by a water moccasin, threw Julie off his back, and stepped on her, breaking three of her ribs. Julie forgave him even as his hooves were striking her chest, and would have forgiven him with her dying breath if he had not ceased his attack, because in Julie's silent philosophy, being angry with a horse for throwing off a rider, and then killing her, was as arbitrary as resenting a bird its flight.

Julie suggested that we play a form of rodeo, which was, I swear, that we each take a running start and jump on Mingo's back, from behind. I mean jump on him from his butt side, where he was most likely to deliver a fatal kick.

I collapsed to the ground, moaning. "Julie," I said, reasonably, "we can't jump on Mingo's back. Look at Anita and Annette. Do you want them to die?"

"Get up, you big nut," Julie said extra quietly, offering me her hand. I took it, and Julie went over and began stroking Mingo's neck. Dana appeared beside me in a cloud of ill will.

"Coward," she hissed gleefully between her teeth. She wanted me to know she knew the truth about me without Julie hearing.

"You go do it, then," I said, waving toward the gray-dappled Mingo, who stood however many hands equals a really tall horse plus three or four more.

Julie started about thirty feet from Mingo, so that by the time she reached him, she was running full out. She put her hands on his haunches and vaulted up onto his back just the way Jesse James would have, in one fluid motion. Mingo never moved, but continued to stare straight ahead, no doubt contemplating the many varieties of horse revenge available to him.

Dana said she would go next. She spit, and then turned and gave me her most smug face.

"I don't even want to watch this," I said, my arms crossed.

"You ought to watch it and learn something," she said, her voice pointedly ironic and manly in the clear autumn air.

"It's your funeral, Dana."

"Yeah, you'll probably be too scared to attend your own funeral, right, Jarvis?" Which brought a little laugh from everyone.

Dana started where Julie had, so that she was running hard when her hands hit Mingo's back. I wish, even now, that I could report that some dreadfully embarrassing but not life-threatening accident had befallen her, but in fact, she vaulted right up onto Mingo's back with just slightly less grace than the inimitable Julie herself. Blessedly, no one else at the party was willing to try it, so I was not alone where I stood, sensibly wary, next to the fence.

Later that same day we were chased by a bull, and as we ran hysterically across the pig lot, my shoes and socks were sucked off by the layers and layers of viscous poop and mud, and we couldn't go back and find them because of the bull. Next: David Lee decided to show us how to do karate, which he had learned from watching late-night television, and naturally requested that I be his assistant. He threw me in an arc by the arm, dislocating it. As I lay on the ground, watching little pinpoints of light explode and fade in my eyes, I heard my father's truck come flying into the barn lot.

As we drove away I could see Debbie in the front yard with her fist raised at David Lee, who had scampered all the way to the top of the big pine tree. He clung to it like a monkey as it swayed. Lying in the emergency room I realized that I never even got to eat any of the homemade french fries or fried mushrooms that Debbie had made. She had cooked so much that she was forced to break out the Fry Granddaddy. Plus I knew for a fact that there were about twenty-five freezing-cold Cokes in the refrigerator, the refrigerator that Julie and I had surprised Debbie by painting with exterior house paint, the same refrigerator on top of which there was a clock that always said 8:30. A party was going on in that kitchen, without me.

DANA INVITED ME DOWN to see their new Ping-Pong table, which her father had set up in the pristine barn.

"Wow," I said, running my hand over its greenness. "Where'd you get it?"

"We were in Muncie last night," Dana said casually, even though it was fairly unusual to find oneself in Muncie, which was big and far away, "and Dad asked if there was a Zayre's around somewhere, and I said, 'A Zayre's. Yeah. Isn't there one on West Jackson Street?' And we drove over there and sure enough, it was right where I thought it was."

I stood with my mouth open, imagining the weird and superhuman power which would allow a fifth-grader to know the name of a street in a city thirty miles from her home. Mooreland had three north/south streets, and I only knew the name of one of them, Broad Street, and I only knew that because I could see the street sign from my own front porch. As for all the little east/west streets, I couldn't imagine they even had names. Saying, "We live in the house next to Minnie Hodson's old house," was surely more efficient than assigning a number to our front door. And since Mooreland had only one of most things (the exception being churches, of which there were three, one for every hundred people), it was also quite simple to say, "We live at the four-way stop sign," or "I'll meet you in front of the hardware store."

I snapped my mouth shut and nodded, as if I knew exactly the Zayre's she was talking about. We played Ping-Pong for a little while, but it didn't go well. I was completely unskilled and Dana played so hard her shots often went right off the table, and so I spent a fair amount of time searching the corners of the barn. (I later discovered that in order to be a good athlete one must care intensely what is happening with a ball, even if one doesn't have possession of it. This was ultimately my failure: my inability to work up a passion for the location of balls.)

We walked out into Dana's side yard, at loose ends.

"What do you want to do now?" Dana asked.

"I don't care. What do you want to do now?"

"I don't care."

We scuffed our feet and looked at the general flatness and order of Dana's yard.

"We could fight," Dana said, with a dangerous tone in her voice.

"Pshhh," I said, with a sigh. "You know I don't fight, Dana, I'm a Quaker."

She circled me. "So?"

"So. I can't. Just drop it." I looked at the ground.

"Well, I can fight," she said, pushing me hard in the chest.

I took a few steps backward, unbalanced, then righted myself. Briefly, my eyes met hers, and I saw that her face was suffused with a dark light, and she was smiling. Before I could say anything, she pushed me again, and I stumbled. We continued in this fashion all the way back to her hedgerow, and when she pushed me into a blackberry bush, I snapped, and came out swinging, blindly.

I guess I must have hit her at least once, although I have no memory of anything but the hectic movement of the sky and the trees, my own heart pounding, and the ground suddenly spinning and rising. Dana had hooked her foot behind my leg and knocked me down. All too briefly we rolled, an equal contest, and then she had me pinned.

I hated to look at her, but I had no choice. Her bottom lip was bleeding, and her hair was tangled up with grass, and we were both breathing heavily.

"Get off me, Dana," I said, furious.

She just continued to stare at me in a fixed and unnerving way.

"*Get off me, Dana.*"

"I don't want to," she said, calmly.

For a few heated moments I had no idea how to respond. All I could do was stare at her and imagine how ridiculous we looked from the street (which was Broad Street, I happened to know), and then I became scared and pushed her off me roughly.

She sat up in the grass as if nothing had happened, until it became clear that I was leaving.

"Where are you going?!"

"I'm going home." I started walking across her yard.

"Oh, really? Well, the next time you're such a psycho I may

just have to kill you!" She was yelling loudly enough for the neighbors to hear.

"Yeah, yeah," I said, waving her off. "Why don't you go bite yourself, you little shit."

It was my first big swear, and as I stomped up the hill and over the railroad tracks, the whole situation made me feel like my stomach was harboring a fugitive. By the time I got home my eyes were burning with tears, and I desperately wanted to go up and just lie down on my bed, but first I had to walk on down to the corner to see if the street my sister lived on had a name, and sure enough, it did: Jefferson.

Dana never apologized, and neither did I, but she was a big enough person to come to my house later that afternoon. I was lying on my bed with my face toward the wall, and I refused to turn over, even after she had said hello.

"Okay, then. I'm just going to sit here on the floor . . . no, no, I'm not going to sit on the floor, because I can't see it. I'm going to sit on this pile of clothes and books and stare at you until you turn around. I'm going to sit here and stare at you through your fan, even though there's a dead mouse in the bottom of it that has been there as long as I've known you, and now it's just a dried-up little skeleton."

I tried not to laugh, and was doing fine until she started to hum. In order to save us both the extreme embarrassment of Dana's broken voice, I turned over, only to find her sitting in a clothes basket, on top of my dirty laundry, wearing a ratty old Beatles wig she had found in the back of her mother's closet. As soon as she met my eyes she broke full-throated into "Band on the Run," her favorite song in the world. To be fair, she probably was no worse a singer than Linda McCartney, though I would never have said that to her face. The day ended with me laughing so hard I thought my appendix would burst. I begged her to stop.

AND THEN ONE DAY, toward the end of the year, Dana didn't come to school, and when I stopped at her house on the way home there was no answer when I knocked. My mom was waiting for me at our house, and told me that the rumor in town was that Dana's parents had had a terrible fight that had escalated into violence, and that Jo had taken Dana and fled town.

"I don't think they're coming back, honey," Mom said, studying my face.

"They have to. This is where Dana lives; it's where all her friends are. Jo can't just take her away like this." I tried to sound reasonable, but my voice was strained.

"I think, actually, that Jo had been planning it for a while. I think that's what the fight was about." She paused a moment. "It wasn't a good home for Dana, sweetheart, and maybe wherever they end up will be better."

"Wherever they end up? You mean nobody knows?"

Mom shook her head. I stared at her a few more seconds, trying to read her face for clues, but it appeared that she really didn't know where they'd gone.

I went out and sat on the porch swing. The street that ran in front of my house was called Charles. If anyone were to ask, I could say that I lived on the corner of Charles and Broad, or else I could say that I lived behind Newman's Marathon, whichever made more sense. At least I had some choices.

Dana's father and brothers stayed in the house for the rest of the year. No one ever really saw them. One Saturday, a few months after she left, I walked down to Dana's house and knocked on the door. I couldn't bear not knowing anything about her. Lou answered the door after what seemed a long time, bleary-eyed and thick with smoke. He just looked at me, unable to imagine what I was doing on his porch. I finally scrumbled up the courage to ask if I could look in Dana's room, to see if I had left an overdue library book there. He stepped back and let me pass by him without a word.

The house was painfully still. Nothing waited on the stairs. When I turned the corner into Dana's room, my throat was so tight I reached up and touched it. The afternoon sun slanted through the big west window, lighting up the dust motes that filled the air.

Her bed was neatly made. In the corner lay the old Beatles wig, and a pair of shoes she had outgrown. A single picture of Shawn Cassidy, cut from a magazine, was still pinned to the wall, but otherwise the room was empty, and rather gray, and looked very like it had when she lived in it. I lay down on the bed a moment, feeling stupid, then got up and went home.

THERE ARE TWO PHOTOGRAPHS, taken at a slumber party at Julie's house, just before Dana disappeared forever. In the first we are trying to form a human pyramid, like cheerleaders. Dana, Anita, Annette, and I are on the bottom, being always the tallest. On top are Rose and Julie and Kirsten. We are laughing wildly into the camera. In the second the pyramid has toppled and we are lying in a heap on the floor, and the expression on our faces is quite different. We are all, in various ways, trying to keep our tender and budding chests from touching the person in front of us, for fear of the sharp knock of pain that accompanied every touch. The days of hard wrestling were already over, although we were just beginning to realize it. From then on, we would spend our lives as girls trying to maintain that flat, sad distance. Some people moved so far away that we never, ever saw them again.

DINER

There are a finite number of times one can safely climb the same tree in a single day; after that point the whole venture becomes meaningless, and potentially dangerous. I had climbed my favorite tree, an oak that had a perfect bottom-shaped well where the big limbs began, about five times. I was getting casual with gravity, and had begun dismounting higher and higher, when I realized that I was aware of my stomach.

I was hungry. I walked into the house, which was so surprisingly empty. My sister had married only a few months before and was now living down the street; my brother was not a person I would consider in such a situation; my father had gone to one of the many mysterious places he had to be; and my mother, who we all trusted for so many years to remain faithfully in her place on the couch, was working.

She had taken a job waitressing at the little restaurant on Broad Street that sat diagonally from the drugstore. From the outside it just looked like a shotgun house. There were even checkered curtains in the window and a front stoop for sitting. Mom had only been working there a few days, and only the lunch shift, but her absence was alarming.

Our kitchen was really a part of our den—separated only by a "breakfast bar" at which no breakfast was ever taken—and I stood in the strange nether world between the den and the kitchen, staring. I never entered the kitchen if I could avoid it, and even as I stood there, deeply worried, I could hear mice skittering around in the oven.

I ran back outside and stood on the front porch, bark dangling from my sweatshirt and my hair. Oh, I was so hungry. I was hungry, hungry, and at what appeared to be a desperate time: the Newmans were not at the gas station, Rose and her family were out of town, and my sister had gone to New Castle. I had no money. I couldn't think of how to steal any. My mom was completely gone.

I sat on the porch steps and contemplated, my stomach growling and grumbling. If I went back in the house I would have to face the kitchen, and if I stayed outside I would surely expire.

I went inside, and slowly, fearfully, walked across the sticky kitchen floor to the refrigerator. The inside of the refrigerator was no better than any other part of the kitchen, but I was able to locate a bag of carrots, which I grabbed, slamming the door behind me. I took them outside and whittled off the grubby outsides with my pocket knife and set to eating them. They were pretty good, for vegetables. I ate one, and then another, and probably a third and fourth, distractedly, until I noticed the whole bag was empty and I wasn't hungry anymore. In fact, my stomach felt like a little carrot rock.

I tried lying down in the yard and moaning out loud, which seemed to comfort the people who died on soap operas. The leaves and twigs snapped and poked in an unfriendly way. When I stood up to head for the house, I found that I felt even worse. I realized I needed my mother.

The walk to the diner was a long and treacherous one. I periodically had to stop and sit down in the grass to gather enough strength to go on. The sun pounded down on me, so that by the time I reached the front door I was stooped over like the emphysemic old man my grandma was married to, Pappy Catt, and I was clutching my stomach. It took all my willpower to straighten up enough to open the restaurant's front door.

Mom was walking out of the back where the desserts were kept, carrying a piece of pie to a man who was sitting at the counter drinking coffee and looking at a map. One look at him told me he was from nowhere near Mooreland. He was wearing a suit, which was, as far as I knew, a habit practiced only by men who sold insurance, like Rose's dad. Mom gestured for me to sit down at the counter, and then she ducked into the kitchen.

Obviously she had not noticed how terribly aggrieved I was. I stooped over to the counter and slid onto the stool right next to the businessman, even though the whole rest of the diner was empty.

He looked down at me without speaking or smiling, then turned back to his map.

My stomach just flat-out somersaulted. I called out, "Mom!"

"I'll be right there!" she yelled back.

I put my head down on my arms and took some deep breaths. When I was able to I shouted again, "Mom! I need some water!"

The man at the counter, perturbed, pushed his water my direction. I sat up straight enough to take a drink, raised the glass to my lips, and vomited, right into the water. What the glass couldn't hold had just fallen neatly on to the counter, and it was nothing but shredded carrots. After I finished making that one last little heave that concludes a throwing up, I found myself quite interested in the contents of the glass, and turned it toward the window to hold it up to the light.

The man next to me dropped his fork in an unnecessarily dramatic way, then grabbed his map and headed for the door, dropping money on the floor on the way out.

My mom came around the corner and saw me looking into the carrot water.

"Oh, sweetheart! What happened?!"

"There was nothing to eat at our house but carrots!" I said, indignant. "So I ate them and got sick and came down here to try and just get a glass of water, and the man sitting there gave me his and I threw up in it. That's the throw-up, right there."

"I see it. Are you feeling better?"

"I feel fine. What kind of pie did I see you carrying earlier?"

Mom felt my head and cleaned up the mess. We both declared that it was one of the more interesting sights we'd ever beheld, and I told her a few more times about how the carrots had just come straight up and so neatly into the glass, like I had planned it. She brought me a piece of warm sugar-cream pie, and it occurred to me that for warm sugar-cream pie I'd throw up every day.

When I stepped out of the restaurant to go home, I noticed that Sammy Bellings was sitting on her front steps next door. I ambled over and sat down next to her. Sammy had blond hair and very slanty cat eyes, and her skin was a brown color. She was one of seventeen kids living in the little house between the diner and an abandoned grocery store; some of the kids belonged only to the father, and some only to the mother, and some had gotten made together, but nobody really knew who was whose. Sammy didn't often wear any panties, so I was quite familiar with her brown bottom. It was something of a scandal at school.

"Hey," she said, waving.

"Hey. I just threw up a bunch of carrots in a glass of water," I told her, pointing toward the restaurant.

"Why did you eat a bunch of carrots?" she asked, wrinkling up her nose.

"Was the only thing I could find. I was starving to death."

"Yeah," she said, nodding sympathetically. "That happened to me once. I was walking around the house saying I'm so hungry I'm so hungry and my ma kept saying I had to wait until dinner, but she hadn't even started dinner. We weren't gonna eat for hours. So I was saying I'm so hungry I'm so hungry and then I found this bag of potato chips and I took them out in the backyard and ate the whole bag and then I puked it all back up and the dog came over and ate it."

Now I didn't know what Sammy meant when she said she went out in the backyard, because what they had was a square of dirt that butted up to the alley, but I didn't say anything. The detail about the dog made the whole story convincing.

"I think moms ought to just feed you when you're hungry," I said, as if I were making a declaration.

Sammy snorted. "Tell that to my mom."

My own mother came out of the front door of the diner, finished with her shift. I saw her and scampered down off Sammy's stoop.

"See ya later!" I said, waving behind me, and she waved back.

I caught up with my mom, who was still wearing her apron with the big pocket in the front. I snuck my hand into it.

"Got any money in here?" I asked, waggling my eyebrows at her.

"You don't need any money," she said, swatting my hands away and pulling me close to her at the same time. "You've got all you need already."

It was an Indian summer afternoon in Indiana, a rare gift. We walked home slowly. I thought Mom might be wrong about me having all I needed, but just at the moment, I had no need to complain.

SLUMBER PARTY

There are only two ways to live your life. One is as
though nothing is a miracle. The other is as though
everything is a miracle.　—ALBERT EINSTEIN

I didn't believe in God, had not ever, as far as
I could remember, believed in God, and yet I
was reluctant to formulate the thought too
clearly, not to mention speak it aloud, for fear
that poor God would hear it and get His feelings hurt.

I believed that the baby Jesus had gotten

born, and that was all lovely. Christmas was my favorite time of the year, in part because of the excellent speech, "Fear not: I bring you good tidings of great joy . . ." and because of the song "The Little Drummer Boy." Anything that involved such persistent percussion was undoubtedly both religious and true.

After he ceased to be a baby Jesus held little interest for me, until he reached the age where he sat for the portrait that hung above the swinging doors in the vestibule of the Mooreland Friends Church. In the painting, which glowed from a fluorescent light bulb hung beneath it, the Big Jesus looks pensive and honey-eyed. His shoulder-length, light-brown hair is as clean and shiny as corn silk, and he has a beautiful tan. He is not scorched like a farmer, but bronzed, like a lifeguard. He is way better looking than either Glen Campbell or Engelbert Humperdinck.

I wanted him to be my boyfriend. My feelings about Jesus didn't alarm me at all, because it appeared that everyone around me was flat-out in love with him, and who wouldn't be? He was good with animals, he loved his mother, and he wasn't afraid of blind people. I didn't buy the bit about his terrible death and resurrection for a minute. I knew, beyond any room for doubt, that nothing in this world is both alive and dead. And this was the thing I most wanted to say in church: if you want him to be alive, you've got to stop hanging him on that cross. But it appeared that the cross was what the people of Mooreland valued above all else—more than his life, more than the sweet way he carried lambs on his shoulders in the pictures on the fans furnished by Main & Frame Funeral Homes—the cross, and the way he got sucked up into heaven to be with the Father who killed him. It was such an objectionable story that I decided to skip it. I decided that Jesus was alive, just as people claimed, and that he lived in the trees around my house. He had picked me out personally, and was following me around, watching my every move. Sometimes I lay out in the back-yard with my blue tape recorder, just holding the microphone up to the sky. I figured if Jesus was ever going to break his long silence, it would be on a warm, breezy day in Mooreland, with his best girl waiting patiently in the grass. The tapes I made were very peculiar and very boring. The only voice heard is that of my dad, telling me he's waiting inside with the Campho-Phenique and the Chig-a-Rid. No one ever tried to discourage me; it is written in our very bones, as a people, that true religion requires sacrifice.

THE ONLY TIME my father entered the Mooreland Friends Church (aside from my sister's wedding) is, fortunately, documented by a photograph. Since Quakers don't believe in sacraments, including baptism, Quaker children, when they're old enough to consent, are instead "dedicated" to the church and the religious life. I was dedicated when I was six years old; I don't remember anyone asking for my permission. Dad dutifully put on his brown suit, which he highlighted sportingly with a pink shirt, and accompanied us to the services. I wore my little yellow dress, and my mom was traditionally Quaker in dark gray. In the photograph we are standing in front of the altar, my mom and I looking fairly pleased, my dad looking defiant. I stand between my two parents, holding the hand of each. After the ceremony was over, our pastor, Eddie, asked if I knew what had just happened, and I said, "Sure. Mommy and Daddy and me just got married to God."

My mom belonged to a prayer cell that met after Wednesday

evening services, and often I would stay and listen to them rather than walk home in the dark by myself. It seemed that the women mostly prayed about their husbands and children, which got them all worked up into a state. I've never seen so much crying as went on in my church; some people cried *every time* they walked through the door. My own mother prayed about almost nothing but my dad. Week after week, year after year, for twenty-seven years she prayed that God would touch his heart and cause him to become a hardworking, nondrinking, churchgoing kind of man.

And every week, when we got home, we would find Dad sitting stone-faced in his chair, watching television with his arms crossed over his chest, smoking cigarettes. It was a romantic way to sit and smoke, I thought. As soon as my mom left the room Dad would ask, "Was my name mentioned?" Not looking at me, but still staring straight ahead.

"Oh, yeah."

"Well, next week you go in there and tell them that they can pray for me till the cows come home, but I'm a stubborn old cuss. They're never going to win."

And I would say okay, but both of us knew that I'd swallow my own tongue before I'd make an announcement to a group of adults at church. Besides, it never crossed my mind that my mom's prayers would be answered. I knew my dad was safe.

MOM USED TO SAY that my dad was a mountain man, which was obviously just a figure of speech, since most of Indiana is flat as a pancake. Her point was that Dad was a wild man, which was certainly true. One year at Thanksgiving we went camping, and in order to cook the turkey over the campfire my dad invented what he called a "turkey tent," a device none of us could replicate, which cooked the turkey perfectly and in record time. I know it will someday show up in an L. L. Bean catalog, patented by someone not even related to me.

He was a great hunter, fisherman, and keeper of bees. He would eat even the most obviously offensive foods, such as possum and fried mush, and was never careless with fire or guns. And I always believed that if he were dropped into a wilderness with just the barest essentials, he would emerge victorious, if for no other reason than he was so blindingly well organized that nature would never stand a chance.

Our little camper was always packed with the greatest care, and nothing was left to chance. All medical, laundry, and culinary emergencies were covered. We had enough decks of cards that we could have easily added sixteen unexpected people on Euchre night, and when one of the lightbulbs blew out in the string of fishlights we hung around the camper, he had an extra, and usually in the right color. If we took a detour he had a map of that town, too. Our dogs never misbehaved, our tires never went flat, and if the people camping next to us needed five gallons of gas, he would just happen to have it. When he was at the wheel, everyone else could sleep, because he never would. In short, he was what it meant to be a father and a man in 1971. Up against his power I could see none of his failings.

ONE EVENING AS WE SAT on the porch swing, generally not talking, just swinging, I asked him.

"Daddy, why ain't you a Christian?"

He gave me the one eyebrow, but without looking at me. "Who says I'm not?"

"Everybody."

"Yeah, well, they're right."

We went on swinging. Sometimes conversations with him only went so far.

THE NEXT MORNING he woke me up pretty early, which made me think we were going fishing, but instead he announced that we were going to his church. Now I could see that this was nothing but a trick, because my dad wouldn't belong to any church that would have him, and it wasn't even Sunday.

"Do I have to wear a dress?" I asked, already miserable.

"Nope. Just pull on your jeans."

When I got out to the truck he was sitting there waiting for me, drinking coffee out of his thermos cup. Dad could sit in the truck so still, with his arm out the window, as if he were already going some-place. I climbed in and up on the box he made for his kids so we could sit as tall as he did. He thought it wasn't right that we couldn't see out the front windshield just because we were small. Danny had used it, then Melinda, but now it was completely mine. The box was wooden, but covered with a pad and then a brown-and-white-checkered cloth. I rode in the middle of the seat, right next to him, which meant I had to all the time move my feet so he could shift gears. There was no such thing as a seat belt in our family.

We drove out of Mooreland and down the highway toward New Castle, and then past New Castle toward the little town of

Dunreith. We didn't get as far as Dunreith, though, before he turned off the highway into a campground called Lake of the Woods. It wasn't a campground we ever stayed in; it was too close to home and too close to the highway, but he drove through it like he knew it, and some of the permanent residents, the people who lived in their little trailers, waved at him in a familiar way.

We wound around all the campsites, and then back a narrow, rutted road that went right into the woods. I kept looking at him, waiting for an explanation, but he was silent. When the road ended, we got out of the truck and followed a well-worn trail. It wasn't long before we had reached a large, round clearing. The perimeter was marked by big logs set in the ground, perfect for sitting. And at the front of the clearing, or what appeared to be the front by the way the eye was drawn to it, was a cross, made from huge, gnarled trees.

Dad sat down on one of the logs, and I sat down next to him.

"This is my church," he said, waving vaguely at the woods surrounding us.

"Daddy, this is a campground."

"So?"

"So it ain't a proper church. This is just where people come when they're away from home. What kind of services do they hold?"

"I don't know. I never come when there are other people here."

"Then that settles it. To have a church you've got to have other people; a preacher; an altar, and some fans for waving when it gets hot."

"Is that all?"

"No. And some hankies. You know Hazel Deckerd? She can

fold up a hankie with her thumb inside so it looks like the swaddling Jesus."

He thought for a moment about how completely I knew a real church. "What does the Bible say about two or three gathered together?" he asked, not like in Sunday school, where everything was a quiz, but like maybe he just forgot.

"'Where two or three are gathered together, there I am also.'"

Dad could sometimes get a smarty-pants look on his face, which I wouldn't have ever been allowed to do myself. It was a look that said that people were just regularly walking into his traps.

"Does it say two or three what?" he asked, looking me in the eye.

I thought. Of course it meant people, but that's not what it said. I shook my head.

"Are there two or three of something out here?" he asked, gesturing around us.

I nodded. "There are two or three trees, and two or three bugs, and two or three flowers. And us, of course."

"Then this is where God is."

I leaned against his arm. He was wrong about the Bible, and I knew it as well as I knew all the books of the New Testament, in order. Christians were flat-out strict about how everything got read, and nothing was to be scrumbled around unless it was by a preacher. But it was a nice place. It was peaceful. I was glad that Dad had a church of his own somewhere. His cigarette smoke hung blue in the air all around us.

WHEN MELINDA WAS IN HIGH SCHOOl she was allowed to have a slumber party; she invited a Jamey, two Debbies, and a Cindy. It was unusual to have friends spend the night in our house. For one thing, my dad couldn't abide a lot of noise, and also our house was just a disgrace, which was a thing I wasn't aware of until the first time I had someone over for the night. It was Rose's younger sister, Maggie. We'd known each other since Maggie was in diapers. She walked into the kitchen and saw a pan of biscuits. She asked me if she could eat one.

"Oh. You'd better not." I looked at them hard, but could not honestly remember how long they'd been sitting there. I thought since maybe Christmas, which had been three months before.

She picked one up and banged it down on the pan. These were obviously excellent weapons, so she threw it at me. We threw those biscuits at each other all over the house. Maggie was such a good sport.

Before the slumber party, my sister cleaned up the house as best she could, making it relatively presentable. I was to stay out of her way and not try to insinuate myself into the party, a thing I often did when her friends came to visit. My best trick was to put on one of Melinda's albums and sing along with every word of a complicated song, like "Along Comes Mary," by the Association. My other favorites were "Every Christian Lion Hearted Man Will Show You," by the Bee Gees, and "Sounds of Silence," by Simon and Garfunkel. I was downright fond of pop music.

"Wow! Do you see what your little sister is doing? She knows the Canticle part of 'Scarborough Fair'!"

"Yes, I see," my sister would say through clenched teeth, trying desperately to heave stink-eye my way.

At the end of the song the girls would clap and ask if I knew another one and I would act terribly shy but would eventually agree and choose Frankie Laine's "Swamp Girl," which was pure poetry and always got everybody scared. Then, with a death grip on their attention, I would perform some headstands on the couch and maybe twirl my baton.

All of my best activities were forbidden at Melinda's party, which put me in a sulk. I refused to just leave and go stay peaceably at Rose's or Julie's. My dad offered to take me down to the drugstore for an ice cream cone, but that wasn't nearly enough of a bribe, so I announced I wouldn't go anywhere with him.

The party arrived and went up to Melinda's bedroom. By standing underneath her window I could hear a lot of what they said, but I didn't know what any of it meant. There was a lot of talk about something being "Rusty," and skinny-dipping, which I assumed was something one did with an uncooked chicken. They mostly laughed, and played Melinda's little record player, which just about caused me to expire from deprivation. They settled down to braid each other's hair and someone started to read from her journal. My mother kept a journal, but she said that if anybody ever read it she'd make that somebody chew off her own hands. It was no idle threat, either: Petey Scroggs starved a rabbit until it ate its own paw. He showed it to me.

UNTIL MY SISTER got married and left home, I didn't really have a proper bedroom. The room next to my sister's, which was really for storage, had a bed in it, and I sometimes slept on that, and in the winter I slept on a cot next to the stove. Mostly I slept on the couch in the living room, in an army-green sleeping bag that had flannel duck hunters inside, rifles raised.

When I lay down on the couch to go to sleep the night of my sister's slumber party, the girls were all still upstairs, and my parents were in the den watching television, behind the heavy curtain that divided the two rooms. I fell asleep on my back and dreamed that a fat green troll was sitting on the arm of the couch running his ugly fingers through my hair, which caused me to wake up mightily disturbed, only to realize that there really was something on the arm of the couch and it really *was* in my hair. I had no option but to scream. My sister and her friends came thundering down the stairs and my parents came running in from the den, and there was my cat, PeeDink, curled up and purring, happily chewing on a big chunk of my hair that was actually still attached to my head.

There were big laughs all around, except from me.

"Stupid cat," I grizzled, glaring at him. "Why would he be wanting to eat my hair, anyway?"

"If you ever washed it you might attract fewer animals," my sister said, much to the enjoyment of her guests.

"Yeah, well *you* wash it," which was no kind of come-back, so I just got in my sleeping bag mad. The chewed part of my hair was damp and smelled like cat food.

My parents went back in the den, but my sister and her pals stayed in the dark living room, whispering. Our living room was quite large, thirty-three feet long and nineteen feet wide, so there was room for all of us, but still. I was trying to sleep.

They gathered down around the window seat. One of them had an idea that the others were disputing, but not heartily. I heard my sister say, "My mom would kill me if she knew," which didn't prevent her from fetching a candle and some matches.

They sat down in a circle not far from the end of the couch where I lay. I couldn't imagine what they were doing, but it was so quiet and whispery that I got tickle-chills on my back. I hoped it would go on all night. They lit the candle, and one of the Debbies, the most brazen of them, began to speak.

"Dublah, Dublah, Dublah! We call you forth from the land beyond," she said, eerily, and after a few seconds of silence, "Call him forth, dummies! We're all supposed to do it!"

And the rest of the girls responded, "Dublah, we call you forth," but they didn't do it much together, and somebody started to giggle.

This went on for a few minutes, Debbie leading and the rest following raggedly behind, and then they fell into a more rhythmical pattern. The candle flickered on the ceiling and on the portrait of my grandmother Mildred when she was sixteen. The portrait was in profile, and I stared at it every evening as I tried to fall asleep, and every evening the lips began to move. I hated that picture. I felt that my grandmother was trying to tell me a terrible secret I didn't want to know. I could, of course, have just asked her if she had some secret, since she only lived in New Castle and had a telephone. In life she was a skinny, sharp, and pinchy woman of little intelligence who had been abusive to my mother. She was loved by none of us. But in portrait, sixteen and beautiful, she was rich and insistent in her strangeness, and I found her much more interesting.

Listening to the whispers at the end of the couch, and looking at my grandmother moving her lips so desperately, I thought of the most frightening picture in the house. It was called *St. Veronica's Handkerchief,* and the artist had painted Jesus's head complete with the crown of thorns and little drops of blood running down. His mouth was slightly open, and his eyes were closed and looked bruised, as if he had been dead for a few days. His eyes were closed, that is, until one took a few steps back from him, and then they opened. They were dull and dark and somehow still dead, and once they opened it was hard to make them close again. I could walk toward the picture and then backward, forward and back, and make Jesus's eyes open and close many times. I could stare at it until *his* lips, too, began to move. On the whole it was one of the most gruesome sights I had ever beheld, which included the chewed-off paw of Petey Scrogg's starved rabbit.

Right in the middle of my reverie I realized what my sister and her friends were doing. They were holding a seance, which was one of the most wicked and wrong things it was possible to do. It was way worse than coveting your neighbor's ass, for instance, because it involved the Devil, who, once he got into your house might never leave, like flying ants. My heart-rate doubled, and I felt like my eyes would fly out of my head. They were calling forth a little dead boy. They were trying to make a little dead boy come sit right on the couch with me.

Across the room from me was a tall skinny window. The top of the window was only a couple feet from the ceiling, which was ten feet high. I found myself looking at the sky, hoping to see the moon, or at least some familiar stars, so I would know I had not sunken into some Devil pit from which there was no hope of return. I knew that if I could only find the strength or the will to call my mother she would come in and break this spell with one fierce wave of her hand, because my mom would simply not abide the Devil in her house, nor any little dead boys, either, but as I was mustering up my courage, I saw him, and not at the foot of the window, on the ground, but at the top, in the trees.

It was not Dublah, the little dead boy, it was Jesus. He was all white and filmy, like Casper, but there was no mistaking his hair or his beard or his long white nightgown. He simply floated there, and looked at me. He didn't beckon with a long skinny ghost finger, and he didn't try to tell me secrets I didn't want to know. We just looked at each other, and his look felt like a holding, like being held and lifted all at once. And that feeling of comfort was so distinct and powerful that I suddenly had the strength to speak.

"I see him!" I whispered, but so powerfully and sharply that it was more like a yell.

The girls froze. They turned as one and looked at me like captured birds, then looked where I was pointing. For just a moment as they turned he hovered there, but then he vanished.

"He was there, at the top of the window, I saw him!" I said, sitting up. The girls leaped up and surrounded me on the couch.

"Who? Who did you see?!" they asked, all talking at once.

"It was Jesus! He came out of the trees! He was in the window!"

They began to laugh, nervously. They told me I had been dreaming, and that Jesus must have been pret-ty tall. I was encouraged to be quiet, so Mom would not come in and ask what the girls had been doing. My sister told me she would get me a new jump rope if I kept the dead boy a secret and I was no fool—I agreed.

But I had to tell; Jesus is not something one can keep a secret, and the next day I told both my parents and my brother. I left out the part about the seance in order to get the jump rope. My sister trusted me to honor a bargain.

No one believed me. Most everyone was kind about it, but it was clear they thought I had been dreaming, or was still overly excited about waking up to find PeeDink in my hair. It didn't matter that I could describe him perfectly, or that I knew I had been awake; it didn't matter that he came out of the trees, just as I had always suspected; Jesus had not appeared in my window.

AT CHURCH THE NEXT WEEK, when it came time to testify, the regulars stood up and thanked God for all the blessings of the week before. Some people asked for the strength to carry their burdens with grace. I shivered inside, hoping my mom would not speak. She often did, on account of how grateful she was for everything, most especially God's love, but this week she just sat still, as if my hard hoping had worked on her and held her to the pew.

Then Hazel Deckerd, a few rows up, stood and said she felt like the Lord was leading us in a day of song, which were my favorite days. I had to nod in agreement, as if the Holy Ghost had spoken to me, too. In our church there were great singers, and on the music days we just stood up and sang one song after another, as people called them out, and the first song Hazel called for was a rouser. By the time we reached the chorus we were singing as one body, swaying and raising our arms in the air. I hoped the God I didn't believe in could hear us, and that somehow the sound would travel out the open windows and down to my yard:

He Lives! He Lives!
Christ Jesus lives today.
He walks with me and talks with me
Along life's narrow way.
He Lives! He Lives!
Salvation to impart.
Don't ask me how I know he lives,
He lives within my heart!

ESP

Dan was not quite three when Melinda was born, and where he had been boisterous, boyish, energetic, and strong-willed, she was placid and curious and sweet. Lindy brought to the world a brand of sympathy that set her apart from other people; my mom used to say that Melinda was like a living, breathing antennae, sensitive to all conditions: animals, people, the weather.

Dan was six, almost seven, and Melinda was four. Mom had been reading, shall we say, quite a bit, and one of her fascinations at the time was with intelligence, particularly the extrasensory variety. In a magazine sent to her by Duke's Institute for Parapsychology she found a children's ESP test, a simple thing involving a screen between the parent and the child, and a group of cards marked with easily identifiable shapes: a sailboat, a ball, a book, a train, and a doll.

Dan went first. Mom explained to him what she was going to do, that she was going to choose one of the five cards and pick it up, then look at him. All he had to do was tell her which one she was holding, and she would keep track of the ones he got right.

She picked up the first card, the sailboat. "Okay, Danny. Now you tell me which card you think I'm holding."

He answered immediately. "The sailboat."

Mom picked up the next card. "Which one this time?"

"The ball."

"And now?"

"The ball again."

Danny guessed correctly the first fifteen times, and then, as Mom remembers it, a look passed over his face, something just faint and flickering, and his next ten guesses were wrong. Fifteen out of twenty-five.

They started over, and in the second round he got two out of twenty-five right, and in the third round he answered them all incorrectly. By the end he would barely look at her, and when she said they were finished he stood up and left without a word. Mom looked at his scores. She tapped her finger on the table. Then Melinda walked in, her eyes full of daylight and the sweet mystery of her personality, and Mom performed the tests without the same intensity she'd given to them for Danny, and Melinda got eighteen out of twenty-five correct the first time; twenty the second time, and on her third attempt she correctly named all twenty-five.

Mom sent them out to play, then consulted the magazine on the results. As she understood it, the law of averages would suggest that most people could get five out of twenty-five correct. Scores above that suggested a telepathic gift; scores below five were also suggestive. What Melinda had done was obvious: she was a receiver. But what Dan had done was more subtle: he was a blocker. He had the gift to guess the answer, and so he refused to give it. Mom put her head down on the table and thought about his other characteristics. He was fiercely stubborn as a baby, and when he got to be a toddler, almost no punishment would work with him. Our doctor suggested that she merely take away, temporarily, something he loved, and the first time she did so, Danny turned on her and said, "I don't want it anymore." She was nervous about what would happen when he entered school.

Melinda's scores, especially, bothered Mother so much she burned the cards. But she continued to test the two of them in small ways. If she looked hard at Melinda's back, for instance, Melinda would turn around almost immediately. But if Mom looked at Danny's back, he stiffened, then left the room.

"SO ARE YOU SAYING Danny and Melinda both had the ESP?" I asked my mom after she told me the story of the test.

"Yes. It's not that simple, but basically, yes."

"Well, then. I must have it, too. Where's those cards? You better test me."

Mom said she had thrown away the original cards, but she

could make some more. We sat down on opposite sides of the dining room table, a bunch of books propped up between us.

"Okay. Do you remember the designs on the cards? A sailboat, a ball, a book, a train, and a doll?"

"Yeah, yeah, go on."

"All right, I'm holding up a card. What is it?"

I thought a moment. "It's a horse."

"Sweetheart. A horse isn't one of the choices."

"Right. It's a big pine tree wavin' in the wind."

"Honey, there are no pine tree cards."

"Oh. Right. It's one of them nasty billy goats with an antler."

Mom sighed, then put her little homemade cards in a pile. She said I'd done really well. I jumped up and ran outside to see if I could melt rocks with just the force of my mind.

INTERIOR DESIGN

Decoupage hit Mooreland pretty hard, as did antiquing, and hand painting one's own ceramics. My dad was especially good at decoupage, and made a number of very beautiful things to hang around the house. My personal favorite was the Bill of Rights, which he burned around the edges and affixed to a large flat piece of cherrywood. He screwed a ring into the top and it hung on the wall in the living room. I used to stand and study it. It survived until one afternoon when Dad was trying to repair the wiring in an outlet below it. At that time we had a cat named Abednego who performed no end of evil tasks, and as Dad knelt there, Abednego went scampering right up Dad's back, using, of course, his claws. Dad raised up in alarm and hit the Bill of Rights, causing it to fall squarely on the back of his head, and before I knew what had happened, Dad had grabbed the plaque and slung it in fury across the room. He missed the cat, but hit the window seat, and the wood cracked in half. Abednego was nowhere to be seen—he was in pursuit of other happinesses, no doubt—so I picked up the wood and tried to fix it, but it was beyond repair.

A few minutes later I heard the cat upstairs in my room, patiently and thoroughly knocking my glass doll collection off my dresser. The dolls came from Avon, and were filled with perfume. The bottom half (which held the cologne) was glass and the top half was plastic, but the two parts were the same color, and made to look like one beautiful, expressive thing. I had a blue girl in a dress holding a basket; an ivory girl in a swing, laughing; a green girl with a lamb; and my personal favorite, a wedding girl.

Dad turned to antiquing, a process by which a new thing was made to look old. In general the technique involved painting an object one color, then putting another coat of paint of a different color over the first and wiping it with a cloth, allowing the first color to show through. His largest project was a heavy ammunition box on wheels that he designed for housing our family photographs. He first painted it a sort of beige color, and followed it with a khaki green. It was very successful. When he was finished, what had originally just been a wooden box now looked like something you might buy at an auction, by accident.

Everyone in town turned on to ceramics at the same time. A

local woman opened a little shop in an abandoned gas station at the south end of town, and it became a popular place to spend an evening. My mom liked painting small, pretty things. For her first grandchild, my niece Jenny, Mom made a bowl that looked like a bed; the top was a rabbit, sound asleep. On one side Mom painted Jenny's name and birth date, and on the other, a quotation from a John Donne poem: "I am a little world made cunningly." She filled it with chocolates and gave it to Jenny for Easter. It was so pretty I wanted to break it.

My dad liked ceramics, too. He painted a plaque for the wall of the den that stayed there for years. It showed a little cowboy, standing with his legs apart, swinging his two six-shooters. The cowboy's hat was pulled down all the way over his eyes. The surface of the plaque was pocked with what appeared to be bullet holes, and it read ANOTHER DAY, SHOT TO HELL.

Debbie Newman was the undisputed master of the hooked rug. She was so advanced that she even designed her own. Over the fireplace in the Newmans' living room was a hooked-rug picture of Big Dave's best horse, the late Navajo. I sometimes sat and watched her at work. Her fat little hands just flew over the surface of the mesh. The hooked rug is made with an apparatus that has a wooden handle and a complicated and cruel-looking hook and lip combination. I could never figure it out, even though Debbie tried to teach me, nicely, a half a dozen times. Julie was no slouch herself when it came to hooking a rug, but she had no patience with me, so I gave up. Julie could also draw and paint very well, and as we got older her paintings began showing up around the house. They were all of horses. Sometimes a cowboy.

Joyce, Rose's mom, could flat-out copy a masterpiece painting.

It was shocking. She would set up an easel, get out her oil paints, choose a painting she liked from a book or magazine, and set to it. Voilà. Within a week there that painting would be, and in this way William and Joyce were able to go even one step farther in making their house the most winning and sophisticated in town. She painted Van Gogh's Sunflowers, an old-timey-looking picture of a boy and girl on either side of a stump, and a young black boy with a bunch of violets. I can't repeat, for its rudeness, the way Joyce referred to this last picture. There was no harm done in saying this word in Mooreland, however, because there was not a single black person within or even near the town's borders, and never had been. All the way up until I was born the signs marking the town limits had borne a warning to anyone of color about the sun setting on them in our town. I'm paraphrasing. Saffer's General Store, which sat empty across Broad Street from our house, had been one of the secret state headquarters for the KKK, back in the 1920s, or so rumor had it. Even so, I was forbidden by my mother from using certain words to designate people of other races. It didn't occur to me to want to; I'd never met a black person.

There was a woman in our church named Rose of Sharon who was so crafty that my mom said she probably crocheted her major kitchen appliances out of steel wool. I went to a baby shower at her house one night. All the women and girls from the church were there, and we each, in the spirit of Quakerism, left the party with a gift. There were no winners. I got a purse, which Rose of Sharon had made out of a plastic butter bowl. She punched holes around the top of the bowl and attached a crocheted top with a drawstring. It was a very clever and handy design for a purse. My mom "won" a doll with a hooped skirt that covered up a roll of toilet paper, and my sister took home a hat that was made from smashed soda cans held together with yarn. Rose of Sharon's entire house was covered with her art, which featured, in addition to knitted things, yards and yards of peach and pink lace attached to the bottom of everything that wasn't moving. R.O.S. had some condition which caused her eyes to bug out so far one could nearly see her brain; my mom suggested it was probably caused from the shock and horror of waking up in that house every day.

A couple of hippies came to town, and took up residence in the row of apartments the Newmans owned across the alley from the gas station. They were interesting to watch. I had never seen hippies in the flesh before, but I knew what to expect of them from watching *Laugh-In*. The guy hippie had a beautiful young Irish setter dog that he kept on a rope all day. It made me crazy. I couldn't imagine what he was thinking; the dog used to get so agitated it looked like she might hang herself. Finally, about a week before Father's Day, I walked over and knocked on their door. The girl answered. All behind her was sweet-smelling smoke. I told her I had been noticing her dog, and I thought it was a shame to keep it tied up like that. As I spoke, the dog spun in wild circles and barked at me, in a friendly way. She told me that they didn't really want the dog, but didn't know what to do with it.

"I'll buy it from you," I said, impulsively.

"I don't know," Hippie Girl said, waving her hand vaguely around her face. "I'll have to ask my boyfriend." She looked at me a long moment, trying to remember who and where her boyfriend was. He was sitting behind her on the couch.

"Come on in," she said, and opened the screen door.

Well. That apartment was a sight. One whole wall was covered with a velvet rug that featured bulldogs in a poker game; on the other wall was a poster of bright swirly colors that made my stomach drop. An American flag covered the window, and they had screwed hooks into the ceiling, from which hung twinkly little pieces of glass that would have caught light if any had been allowed in. There were posters of men with guitars, and cartoon women with big, visible breasts. Aside from the sprung sofa and an old television on a rusted, rolling stand, the only furniture was a toilet that was filled with dirt. Plants were growing in it. A little whistle came out through my teeth.

"You want my dog?" The young man on the sofa was hardly visible through the screen of smoke, but his voice was slow and harmless.

"I'd like to take her. Sure," I said, craning my neck to see into the kitchen.

"How much you give me?"

"I don't have any money. I'll have to trade you something."

"Well, what have you got to trade?"

"What do you need?"

This stopped him. He looked at Hippie Girl, and swaying, she looked back at him.

"We could both use a haircut."

"Okay. I'll cut your hair. Then I get the dog free and clear, right?"

"Yep."

I went home to get some scissors. I'd never cut anybody's hair before. I wasn't even the type to cut the hair off my dolls, the way some of my friends seemed compelled to do. I had whacked off chunks of my own hair before, but only because they were bothering me, and certainly not by any design, but a dog is a dog.

When I got back to the hippie apartment, they were sitting outside in the sun, leisurely. Hippie Girl had brought out a bowl of water and a comb. I took them back to my house and had them sit on the little wall around our front yard. I did the girl first, who seemed hypnotized by the sunshine and by my combing her hair. Her hair was pretty clean but she smelled sweet and funny. She wore a thin flowered skirt and a top so small I would have used it as an undershirt. I decided I loved her. I just cut around on her hair, some here, some there, and then told her she was done.

Hippie Guy wasn't wearing a shirt, and there was hardly anything sticking to his ribs. I thought about offering him some free oatmeal, but his long, long hair distracted me. I combed it, then got it wet, then just cut a straight line along the bottom, taking off about an inch. He had a bushy beard that nearly covered his mouth, making it look like a cave. I asked would he like me to cut off some of his beard and he said sure, so I cut around on that, too, then told him he was done.

We walked back to their apartment and they told me, without checking, that I had done a fabulous job on their hair. They said the dog's name was Janis, but that I could call her what I wanted. I asked would they keep her till Father's Day and they said sure.

On Father's Day morning I went and fetched Janis with a piece of rope. She drug me halfway to the bank before I got her under any kind of control, and even then I was holding on for dear life and all the muscles in my skinny arms were quivering. Dad was in the house, wondering why I wasn't getting ready for church. I popped my head in the door and yelled for him to come out on the porch and when he did, there we were, Janis leaping up into the air and running up and down the steps, her red feathers flying, and me rag dolling around behind her.

"Happy Father's Day!" I yelled, just before she slammed me into one of the porch posts.

"Zip?" Dad said in a curious and cautious way, flipping his cigarette into the yard in the expert way he had as he stepped out onto the porch.

"This is your dog! I got her just for you!" I said, sailing past him and landing on my knees in the yard.

He walked out and took the rope from my hands, which were red and raw, and pulled Janis to him gently. As soon as she saw him she sat down and looked him in the eye. Her face was so beautiful and narrow she could have been a red-haired girl, looking at him the way she was. He rubbed the top of her soft head and behind her ears. Janis's eyes narrowed and nearly closed. She and I were both out of breath.

"Happy Father's Day," I said again, but quietly and more worried.

For a moment he didn't say anything, then he looked up at me. My dad was not a crying man, but his eyes were bright with tears.

"Thank you."

"You're welcome," I said, staring at the ground.

"I think I'll just call her Red, if that's okay."

"That's a really good name," I said, reaching out to touch the bones on the top of her head. She was so beautifully made I felt like I was touching a newborn baby. They were inseparable for the next fourteen years.

———

THE WHOLE THING FINALLY GOT to me and I complained to my mom that I couldn't do a single, stupid kind of craft. I was the worst. She and Dad conferred and then brought me home a paint-by-numbers set. I went to town on it. In the next few weeks I painted Sad Clown, Bronco Rider, and Lake With Evergreen Trees. They were breathtaking, especially from a distance. We hung them all over the house. I chose to put Sad Clown in the den, right next to my dad's gun rack. Up against the wood paneling it was nothing but fine art.

CEMETERY

At the beginning of my ninth summer it became clear that I had outgrown my bicycle. My body was so long and coltish that my knees had begun to hit the handle bars when I pedaled, and the bike had developed some squeaks and whines that I couldn't calm, even after spraying nearly the whole thing with WD-40. My dad finally noticed, and mentioned that it might be time to move up to a bigger bike.

"Would you like to build one yourself?" he asked, squatting in the grass beside me, where I was drenching the chain.

"Build a bicycle?" I couldn't believe such a thing was possible. It seemed as though bicycles just *came* built.

"We could do it, if you want to."

I put down the oil can and gave him my full attention. "Does this involve tools?" I was all the time trying to finagle a way to get my hands on some tools.

"Maybe quite a few of them," he said, knowing that I was sold.

We started out with an old frame he picked up somewhere, and it was literally just a skeleton. It had no handle bars, no tires, no seat, no chain, and the paint left on it was a color that has yet to be signified with a name. The metal tubes that made up the frame were large enough to supply water to a major metropolitan area.

"Jeez, Daddy," I said when I saw it, "this is going to be a big bike."

"Well, it's going to be a fat one."

All the bolts in the frame had to be replaced, and that involved tools. Then we derusted it, cleaned it, and painted it. Paint is almost like a tool. I chose a bright, cobalt blue. If I was going to have a grown-up bike, I wanted a grown-up color. My beloved rodeo bike was lavender, with a purple sparkly banana seat. It was obviously intended for a much younger audience.

The black saddle seat went on with maybe two or three different tools, and then there were the handle bars and the big fat tires. I won't even begin to describe the application of the chain. I was euphoric.

My one concession to the child I had been were brightly colored streamers from the handle bars, my argument being that without them I couldn't tell how fast I was going, which my dad thought was slick thinking. We also added an aaa-ooo-ga horn with a big rubber bulb, and an easily removable metal basket on the front.

On the day we finished it, Dad and I stood back and admired our work. It was a beautiful bicycle. I would never be able to lift it, but it was beautiful. I was ready to roll.

NOW EVEN THOUGH my mother almost never left the couch, she was a woman of many gifts, my favorite being her ability to make anything she was eating crunch. I still don't know how she did it, and I tried to stump her with a wide variety of foods.

"Aha! Try these *raisins*," I would say, triumphantly.

And she'd put a couple of raisins in her mouth and crunch, crunch, crunch. She could make them sound like corn nuts.

"Okay, what about this applesauce cake?"

Into her mouth. Crunch.

"Do you have some kind of trick teeth?" I asked her, but she said no, so I made her open her mouth and show me. It appeared that, remarkably, they were normal.

"Your teeth sure are little," I said, peering in at back teeth that were half the size of mine.

"That's because I have a very small mouth. My bones are also small; I'm really quite a delicately built person," she said, tilting her head in a girlish way.

I patted her on the arm, indulgently. My mother's delicacy was a part of her character she had adamantly clung to over the years, even as her occupation of not moving from the couch softened her and made her, well, motherly. I once heard her tell a friend that she was, in fact, a 120-pound woman, but she kept herself wrapped in fat in order to prevent bruising.

"Have you seen my new bicycle?"

"I did see it. It's very impressive. I'm wondering what you're going to do with your old one; I was thinking that maybe we might give it to some less fortunate . . ."

"I'll tell you the Less Fortunate Child I'm going to donate my bike to, she's sitting right here on the couch with you, so don't even start with me," I said, raising my hand in the universal symbol for stop. "That bike would die without me."

"Hmmm," she said, nodding. "Where are you going to put it?"

"I'm going to lean it up against Dad's tool shed, and I was thinking I might plant some zinnias around it, and maybe I'll make some little sign I can sit up in front of it so people walking by will know, you know. What kind of a great bike it was."

"Like a shrine, you mean," Mom said, blatantly trying to teach me a new word.

"Yes, like a Shrine." As far as I knew, Shrines wore absurd hats and drove miniature cars in circles during the Mooreland Fair Parade, and were praised, inexplicably, for burning children. Although actually, if I was perfectly honest, I could think of a couple kids who could use a good frying.

MY MOM AND DAD never fought, not really, which was a good thing, because my dad had a wicked, wicked bad temper, and if he'd married a woman who fought him they probably would have killed each other. There was a great, legendary moment between them, though, which I'd heard about all my life.

One of the architectural marvels that was my house in Moore-land was my parents' bedroom door, which was solid wood and heavy, and had a porcelain doorknob. It opened into the bedroom. At a forty-five-degree angle from the bedroom door was the closet door, which was solid wood and heavy, and had a porcelain door-knob. It also opened into the bedroom. If the closet door was open, the bedroom door could not be; if they were both halfway open the doorknobs clinked together like little figurines in a rummage sale. It was possible, I had discovered through much trial and error, to get the doorknobs stuck together with neither door open enough to accommodate a grown person. Blocking the door in such a creative way was part of my mental plan for when and if the vampires came.

My mom was nine months pregnant for me, and hugely so, and she and my father were having an actual, vocal argument in their bedroom. My sister's friend Terri was visiting, and the two of them and my brother were all in the living room. The argument reached some critical phase and Mom walked out of the bedroom at the same moment that Dad decided to go in the closet, which caused the bedroom door to smack my mother in the back. She became so instantly enraged (she claimed it was pregnancy that did it) that she waited just a moment until she was sure Dad was halfway into the closet, and then she threw the bedroom door open, which sent my father flying headfirst into the closet about sixty-four miles an hour, all the way back to where we kept the paint cans. My sister said they could hear him tumbling against the cans, and could actually discern the thick moment when he gathered himself up and prepared to face my mother.

He came out of the bedroom like a bullet, red-faced and with his eyebrows riding up his forehead. Mother was standing in the middle of the living room with her hands on her former hips, waiting for him. Melinda and Danny and Terri fled so quickly, and in so many different directions, that Mom later claimed they must have evaporated into the walls. Dad finally came to a stop right in Mother's face, nose to nose, panting like a bull, with his fists clenched.

"Are you going to *hit* me?!?" my mother asked, pressing her forehead more aggressively into his. And before he could answer, she arced out her own arm and slapped his right cheek, hard. He pulled away from her slightly, stunned.

"I said, are you going to hit me?!" and she raised her left arm, and got him on the other cheek, like a good Christian.

Miraculously, he walked away from her. Looking no less deranged or murderous, he backed out of the house without taking his eyes off her; got in his truck and drove away.

It became one of the touchstone moments of their marriage, and afterward, there was never a threat of violence between them again. Mom told me, when I was old enough to ask, that she had learned the lesson from Mom Mary, Dad's mother, who took her future daughter-in-law aside and told her that a woman has got to make herself absolutely clear, and early on. In Mom Mary's own case, she waited until she and my grandfather Anthel were just home from their honeymoon, and then sat him down and told him this: "Honey, I know you like to take a drink, and that's all right, but be forewarned that I ain't your maid and I ain't your punching-bag, and if you ever raise your hand to me you'd best kill me. Because otherwise I'll wait till you're asleep; sew you into the bed; and beat you to death with a frying pan." Until he died, I am told, my grandfather was a gentle man.

SOMETHING HAD BEEN ON THE RISE with my mom for a few months. There were many tearful meetings of her prayer cell, and at least half a dozen thrown-down fleeces (bargains made with God) and phone calls and arrangements. One of her fleeces involved a television commercial of Abraham Lincoln in a classroom. He was standing at a podium saying if I was thinking of going back to college, did I know that I could test out of some required courses by signing up for the CLEP Test, which stood for College Level Entrance Placement. This was all news to me. I heard Mom talk to her women at church about that commercial, and an agreement was reached: if she saw it on the following Friday, anytime before 6:00 P.M., she would call the number on the screen.

On that Friday, although I didn't know why we were waiting for it or what it would mean if she called, I spent the whole afternoon nervously watching TV with Mom. Dad was gone, so it was just the two of us. Three o'clock came and went, and then four, and five, and mom sunk deeper and deeper into a heavy silence punctuated with heartbroken little sighs, because a fleece thrown down is an unbreakable contract. At 5:55 she got up and went into the kitchen and stood holding onto the sink, as if she might throw up. At 5:57, she bowed her head. At 5:58 she looked up, as if she had come to a decision, or was constructing a new shelter made of resignation. At 5:59 I felt my own throat swell with empathy, and at 5:59 and 30 seconds, Abraham Lincoln walked across the classroom that would become my mother's life, and when I looked up at her, she was staring at the television screen with her eyes wide and her mouth open and I knew that what I was witnessing was no less than a miracle.

THE SHRINE TO MY first bike was progressing well. Dad had given me a nice piece of wood on which I'd painted in white "Good Old Bicycle." I was out planting zinnia seeds in a half circle around it when I heard a small commotion in the house. I dropped my spade and ran in to investigate.

Dad was stalking through the house, slamming doors, and my mom was opening every one he shut, following behind him, saying insistently, "But you *promised* you'd build them," and "You promised six months ago," and more variations on what I knew immediately was the Closet Crisis.

Contrary to popular opinion, my dad was not a lazy man. He was not lazy at all, for instance, when it came to Going Places In His Truck. He was also very industrious about Preparing To Go Camping. And if something really interested him, he would work on it all day. He was not, however, interested in working on our house, and so there were, hypothetically, some promises that got made but didn't get kept. Ordinarily my mom just sunk deeper into her corner of the couch and ignored it. She had successfully ignored a quarter of a century of entropy and decay, had sat peacefully crunching popcorn and drinking soda while the house fell down around us. If I had to guess the number of books she read during that time, I would place the number at somewhere in the neighborhood of forty thousand.

For some mysterious reason, she had risen from the couch and taken a stand about the double closet he promised her he would build in the bedroom, and Dad was not a man one took a stand against.

I stood in the doorway, watching him slamming around looking dangerous, and Mom following him looking stubborn. There was nowhere for this to go but worse. I thought we were all saved when he reached for the pile of Dad Stuff that always lay on the dining table off of which no one ever ate: keys, gun, cigarettes, Chap Stick, breath mints. He was going to leave ("Don't go away mad!" my mom used to say cheerfully, one of the many aphorisms that guided her life) in a fury, spinning his tires and throwing dirt up onto the trees, and then come home many hours later as if nothing had happened. But Mom, with some kind of Quaker death wish, stopped him.

"Oh, no. No, you don't. You always, always get to walk out on me, but not this time." She spun around and headed for the door. I scooted out of the way, trying to figure out how on earth she was going to make a dramatic exit when she didn't have either a driver's license or a car.

She stalked past me as if she couldn't see me, down the front walk and onto the sidewalk, where she stopped only long enough to climb onto my new bicycle.

"Um. Mom? That's my new bike? I've hardly ridden it?" But

she was already figuring out the pedals. I could see her mind and her body synchronizing in the way that is the ultimate truth about remembering, the way we carry our memories all through us.

Dad and I ran down the sidewalk to watch her progress. When she got to the corner she turned and headed north, toward the cemetery, which was a very smart move on her part. I also loved riding in the cemetery; the curving lanes were flat and well tended, and there was shade and quiet, and on an autumn day like this one, there was no better place to be.

"Well, she's lost her mind," Dad said, crossing his arms.

But I couldn't answer. All I could see was my mother's delicate body completely engulfing my new black saddle seat. I watched her back grow smaller and smaller as she pedaled stubbornly down the street with a strength no one knew she had, and I thought, clearly, *it won't be long now*.

DRIFT AWAY

My brother could read before he started first grade. But his first-grade teacher, Agnes Johnson, who hated all children from poor families, told him he was stupid in the first week of school, and afterward he decided he couldn't read and would never learn. Listening to stories about him, when he was a great big teenager boy and I was a little girl, it seemed to me that all the stories were marked by that same characteristic: a person in his orbit—a teacher, my sister, our parents—said or did something to him and Danny made a lightning-quick judgment about what his response would be and then stuck with it, even if it had been flat-out foolhardy.

"You mean to tell me," I said, pointing my finger in the rudest way at my mom, "that he went through the second grade and the third grade and the fourth grade," and then I undoubtedly named every single grade, as my mom sat still and very politely acted as if she were listening, "without knowin' how to read?"

"Yes, that does seem to be the case," she answered.

"Hmmmm." I was thinking maybe I could get through school without learning to do a whole bunch of stuff. "How?"

"Well, sweetheart, he was tall. He started playing basketball in the fourth grade, and I think his teachers would have passed him no matter what he did or didn't do. I used to spend hours trying to teach him to read, but he would just go stiff and silent, and I could see that I wasn't getting through."

"I see. So if a person was to go to school and what she really wanted to do all day was run around outside and then come in for lunch, the teachers would just send her on to the next grade?"

"It depends. Are you going to be a high school basketball star?"

"Probly," I said, scratching at a scab. "I'm pretty good already."

WHEN DAN GOT TO HIGH SCHOOL, he had a single teacher who reached out to him, his science teacher, Mr. McCutcheon. One day after class Mr. McCutcheon said to Dan, very kindly, that perhaps high school would be easier if he learned how to read. Dan came home that night, and while Mom was in the kitchen making dinner, he sat in the den and talked to her over the breakfast bar at which no breakfast was ever eaten. He asked her what was on television that night, which surprised Mom, because one of the ways Dan had compensated for not reading was by memorizing things like schedules very, very quickly, in a nearly photographic way.

She said, "I don't know what's on tonight. We all rely on you to tell us."

"Here," Danny said, picking up *TV Guide*. "I'll just check and see."

And as Mom froze in the kitchen, a package of hamburger clammy in her hands, Dan opened the page to Thursday and read her the night's options, along with the plot synopses.

When he was finished, Mom said to him, her eyes filled with tears, "Danny?"

"Mr. McCutcheon said school would be easier if I learned to read," he answered, continuing to flip the pages of the magazine.

"Ah."

"So I just went ahead and did that." He looked up and saw her crying. "Mom? Are you mad at me?"

"No. No, I'm not mad." That was all she said. He wouldn't have allowed her to say much more. He didn't hold much with displays or congratulations. But he read a lot after that. He was, as it turned out, a very, very smart boy.

BY THE TIME I KNEW HIM, everything my brother did required the same ramrod-stiff posture. He sang in a Christian band. He belonged to the Fellowship of Christian Athletes; played drums in the marching band; and was on the varsity basketball team. In photographs of him at seventeen and eighteen he is always at the back of the group (because he was so tall), and whether he was wearing his snare drum or his basketball uniform, his posture belies the truth: he looked like a tree that had grown straight up into the sky without the least impediment.

He was like a tree, but there was also a great deal in him that was stone. With Mr. McCutcheon he started a fossil collection, which eventually took up most of his bedroom. They looked for all the world like gray, dusty rocks to me, but he saw something of a vanished world in them. He had a stony stare. On his basketball team his nickname was "Killer," and he was often sent in at critical points of the game with the sole purpose of seriously fouling an opponent. By the time he was a junior in high school, it was clear that he had made an intractable commitment to religion, and not really to the God of love, the New Testament God who came to earth as a vulnerable man to love the little sheeps, but to Yahweh, the just and mighty. Heaven help the sinner who stood before a mob that contained my brother; if there'd been a first stone to throw, he'd have thrown it.

I didn't know what to make of him. He wasn't my friend and he wasn't my enemy. Dan and Melinda shared a certain wickedness that was often directed at me, and I asked for it, by being so funny-looking and skinny, and by living in the same house with them. One of their favorite activities was placing me in a rocking chair we had that could turn all the way around, and spinning it as fast it would go for a minute or two. Then Danny would lift me out and make me stand up. My eyes would jiggle back and forth in my head in a way that particularly amused them, and when I tried to walk I looked less like a drunk than like a brain-damaged little marionette. Danny had, over the course of my life, lifted me off the floor by my neck, my ears, the straps of my bib-overalls, my feet, my thumbs, my armpits, and my shirt front. If there'd been a scruff to my neck he'd have hauled me up by that, too. In photographs of the three of us, taken before events or at Christmas, I am often looking at him as if I adore him. But I can't remember now whether I really did, or if I was just trying to keep an eye on him; if I was trying to guess from which direction he was going to swoop, how much it would hurt, and if whatever he had planned for me would finally, as he and Melinda loved to threaten, cause me to swallow my tongue.

I must have loved him; I know he moved me. For a while I had a bed in the room between his and Melinda's. I was never allowed in Dan's room, although I was sorely tempted. Everything in there was gray; the wallpaper was faded to gray; there were all those rocks. Above his bed he had an old print of a wolf howling alone on a winter hill, and everything surrounding the wolf, the sky, the ground, had faded to gray. Dan kept all his hunting rifles propped in a row against one wall, and the whole room was laced with traps, including some large enough for a badger. The traps were actually *set,* which meant, I was assured more than once, that they were all just waiting for a skinny little arm or leg. So I never ventured farther than the door.

But at night, during those months my room was next to his, I used to lie with my ear pressed against the wall, listening to him listening to his record player. I loved his taste in music, Glen Campbell, Glenn Yarborough, Roger Miller. But one night he played a record I'd never heard before, and he played it over and over. I'd never heard anything like it—the mournfulness of it that was also thrilling. I got out of bed and lay down in front of his door until I could make out the chorus: "Give me the beat, boys, and free my soul / I want to get lost in the rock and roll, and drift away." He must have played it four or five times, and then he started to sing with it in his clear, deep baritone I was used to hearing ring out only in church. I lay there on the floor listening until he turned off his lights and went to sleep.

BLUE RIVER VALLEY ELEMENTARY
SCHOOL #1

GRADE 4

1974   1975

READING LIST

When the generation just before mine was
growing up, Mooreland was so small that the
elementary, junior high, and high school
grades all fit into the same building. By the
time I started school, the town's school-age
population had grown so much that we had to
hold our kindergarten and fourth grade classes
in a little free-standing building, kindergarten
on one side and fourth on the other. So I went
to kindergarten on the north side of it, then
moved into the big, old school for second and
third grades, back out to the south side of the

shed for fourth grade, into the old school for fifth and sixth grades, and all the way down the highway for junior high and high school.

My fourth-grade teacher was named Mrs. Denver. She collected yogurt cartons for fun and was the most intellectually free of all the teachers I'd had so far. For instance, when the word *caviar* appeared in a story we were reading and she didn't know what it meant, she didn't try to hide it or lie. She asked me if I knew and I lied and told her it was a kind of Alaskan cookie that no one knew how to make anymore, and she simply thanked me.

Mrs. Denver made us memorize and recite poetry, another thing I'd never experienced. The first poem I chose was Frost's "Stopping by Woods on a Snowy Evening," and when I stood up to recite it I got through it marvelously, right up until the last line, "and miles to go before I sleep," repeats itself, and then I got intensely moved and just had to stand there with my throat aching while thirty-seven unsympathetic eyes stared at me. Finally I just ran over to my desk and put my head down, and Mrs. Denver walked over behind my desk and put her hand on my shoulder. The rest of the room stayed blisteringly silent.

"Why does he do that?" I asked in a tight, mad voice, meaning why does he repeat the last line in that devilish way.

"Well, dear, I'm sure it has something to do with poetry, but I don't know what. Why don't you ask your mother." She patted my shoulder for a second, and then asked someone to stand up and repeat their little James Whitcomb Riley gem, and the attention was off me for a while but I felt disgruntled all day.

When I got home I went straight to my mom and asked just what the heck Robert Frost was up to. By this time she had a huge cardboard box next to the couch filled with books from the bookmobile, which she picked up and devoured and tossed back in. If she went through all of them before the bus came back, she just started over.

I told her about how mad I was about "Stopping by Woods," and told her what Mrs. Denver said about poetry, and the mystery of the repeating lines.

Mom thought for a moment about how to explain it. "The best answer I can give is that poetry is all about the effect it has on a reader, and Robert Frost was very, very good at that. If you're asking what it *means* that the line is repeated, I'd have to say I don't know. It's stylistic. But the effect is pretty clear."

"Doggone right the effect is pretty clear! The effect is I looked like an idiot in front of my whole class and I'm never reading poetry again unless it's by James Whitcomb Riley!" And I went storming out of the house to try and shake off the injury done to me with words.

MRS. O'DELL WAS an assistant teacher at our school even when my brother and sister were little, and by the time I was in the fourth grade it seemed she was as inevitable as the moon. She was so old I was always expecting some record book to come and snatch her and make her a star. Even though we were way too grown up for it, she sometimes still sat us in a circle and read us a book or told us a story, and I always sat as close to her as possible, so that I could pinch her on her knuckles. Her fingers were like little basset hounds—they had about a foot of extra skin—and if I pulled up a small hill of skin it would just stay there for probably five minutes. It hypnotized me. Sometimes she just really nicely let me do it and sometimes she smacked me, but I was always willing to take my chances.

Once in a while I left my house for school really early, not even waiting for Rose to come and walk with me, on the off chance that I might get safely past Edythe's house before she left on her march to the post office. There were a few places on the way to school that were good for dawdling, but sometimes, if it was cold, I just went on into the classroom and snuck peeks at Mrs. Denver's poetry books. She had quite a wide variety of collections, all of which had been donated by a library some thirty miles away. I hated them. I wanted to burn them all in the monstrous and terrifying incinerator in the basement of the big school. If I had actually tried to damage a book, however, my very cells would have rebelled, and so I had to content myself with giving the poems scowling looks. Most of Mrs. Denver's collections were just dreadful, full of poems by the likes of Edgar R. Guest and Helen Steiner Rice, but sometimes I would come across a line like "'I am half sick of shadows,' said/The Lady of Shalott," which would send me reeling. The first time I came across Emily Dickinson it was the poem "I am nobody/who are you?" I thought it was a stupid little nonsense poem like in a Golden Book and I just skipped it and then a few pages later I read the line "Dare you see a soul at the white heat?" which caused my tongue to dry up like an old fish. I decided that Emily Dickinson was a lot like Edythe, and I added her to the list of poets I would never read again because of their evil natures.

One morning I snuck in the school through the empty kindergarten room, and I was just about to open the door to the fourth grade when I heard crying and a low voice on the other side. I stopped and looked around for a spy object, but all I could find was a stack of empty yogurt containers, so I used one of those as a listening cup. It was Mrs. O'Dell, and she was comforting someone who was crying brokenheartedly. I lay down on the floor and tried to get one of my eyeballs under the crack, but all I could see was the indoor/outdoor carpeting my mom said looked like a nasty bruise. Unable to bear it any longer, I opened the door just the tiniest crack, just enough to see Mrs. O'Dell holding the hands of a girl named Polly who had been in my grade since kindergarten, but I didn't know at all. I believe that the moment I saw Mrs. O'Dell comforting her was the first time I ever noticed that Polly existed. And here she was, not just existing, but weeping her eyes out over something undoubtedly huge and getting patted by the incredibly old hands of Mrs. O'Dell, which I actually and secretly considered my personal property.

I heard Mrs. O. say, "Do you know when the trial will start?"

And Polly answered, with profound amounts of snot, "I don't know! Soon! And that's [choke] the worst part! That everyone will read about it in the paper today and be talking about it! It makes me sick!"

I thought: in the paper, which meant the *New Castle Courier-Times.* The story of Polly (whoever she is) will be In The Paper, and all I have to do to solve this mystery is find a newspaper and read it. Then Mrs. Denver arrived and I had to quick go out to her car and help her lug in her big easel so she wouldn't know I'd been snooping with one of her yogurt containers. She often propped a big notepad on the easel with things she wanted us to write down, and today's lesson was going to be on Indiana History, a subject she was crazy for. She had written in purple magic marker:

The capital of Indiana is:	INDIANAPOLIS
Indiana was made a state in:	1816
Our Governor is:	OTIS BOWEN
One of our senators is:	BIRCH BAYH

I felt like this was probably the extent of her knowledge of Indiana History, and it was plenty for me. My dad was always trying to tell me about the Delaware Indians, and the Hopewell tribe, and someone called Little Turtle, but all those Indian stories seemed to be about the Indians getting the sham, which seemed ridiculous when I knew from the movies I watched with Julie that Indians were the most excellent creatures anywhere who never got shammed by anybody.

I very busily set up the easel and the Indiana History. Polly had locked herself in the bathroom, and I could hear her making very upset and dramatic post-crying sounds. Mrs. O'Dell was conferring with Mrs. Denver in a loud whisper. Mrs. O'Dell's dentures weren't the most seamless fit, and sometimes she looked like she was grimacing when in fact she just couldn't get her lips all the way down, and sometimes when she talked it looked like the left side of her dentures were about to get away. Plus when she got excited she thrust her head forward like a turtle, and today everything was going wrong at once. She was spitting and her dentures were flapping and her head was bobbing around at about the level of her chest, and the total effect of it caused me to forget to listen to what she was saying. Soon other students began to arrive, and it was time to start another day of fourth grade.

That afternoon I went flying home to read the paper, but my mom had put it down for the dogs, who had already seen fit to employ it. I tried to read it anyway, until Mom caught me and made me go wash my hands. I asked her from the bathroom if she knew any story about Polly or Polly's family, but she said she didn't. I asked her to think a little harder. I asked her to tell me what was on every single page of the paper, but she claimed to only remember one comic and a pattern for a sweater vest, which I knew to be false, because she never read the comics.

I went into the living room and practiced headstands. I tried and tried to think of who might have a paper. The Newmans didn't take a newspaper. They were not so much a reading family, so there was no use heading over to the gas station. Rose's parents took some weird newspaper that wasn't local, which didn't make a lick of sense to me, because they couldn't even check the basketball scores. Rose herself was completely moony over a book called *Jane Eyre.* Even the cover of it was a powerful irritant, and every time she brought it up I left the room, feigning nausea. My dad read only *Walden* and the *Foxfire* books. My mother read anything she could see, but mostly put the newspaper to some practical use. My brother was strict about reading only the Old Testament and *TV Guide.* The last book I could remember my sister reading was *Macbeth,* her senior year in high school.

I thought maybe the drugstore might have a newspaper, so I went flying down there on my bicycle. The front door of the drugstore was very tall and heavy, and where the top of the door met the frame Doc Holiday had hung some sleigh bells which rang festively anytime someone entered. No one was getting the draw on Doc.

When I burst in he was wiping up a milkshake puddle off the counter.

"Doc!" I yelled, closing the door too hard behind me. "I need a *Courier-Times*!"

He turned vaguely in my direction but continued looking at the counter. When Doc shouted the yell came up from his belly and just kind of burst out of his mouth. "Sold out! Don't walk in here yelling! And if you're not going to buy anything, go home!"

I sat down dejectedly at the counter. "Doc, did you happen to read the paper?"

"Nope," he barked, washing out some glasses.

"Because I kind of need to know about something that was in the paper today."

"Well, what are you telling me for?! Do you want anything or not?" This was one of the longest conversations I'd ever had with Doc, and it was obviously testing his patience, so I ordered a lemon phosphate.

I rode around town for a while, surreptitiously checking yards for stray papers, but the only one I found and successfully stole was two days old and soggy, so I put it back and headed on home.

Dad was just getting out of his truck when I rode up. My dad! Of course. He knew everything that happened around Mooreland, so even if he hadn't seen the paper he'd know the story.

"Dad, Dad, Dad, hey. I need to ask you something. Did you read the *Courier* today and do you know Polly who's in my grade and what happened to her that would be in the paper and make her cry? I'm just asking." He was straightening up his front seat and getting ready to flip his cigarette at Edythe's house.

"'Hello, Father,'" he said, "'I'm so glad you're home.'"

"Yeah, yeah. Did you read the paper or not? Because Mom put ours down for the dogs."

"Yes, I read the paper. It's not Polly, it's her older brother, and no, I'm not going to tell you about it because it's not a story intended for your ears. Put your bicycle on the porch if you're done with it."

I rode my bike around and left it on the sidewalk. "Not a story for my ears?! Now what kind of a story is that? I know about the time you and your buddies got drunk at Delco and hid in those big barrels and then accidentally fell asleep clear into the next shift." I had my hands on my hips, giving him the what-for.

"I didn't know you were listening when I was telling that story."

The truth was I wasn't just listening, I was hiding behind the couch and recording it on my little blue tape recorder, but I wasn't about to tell him that.

He walked past me on up to the front door. He held it open like a gentleman.

"You coming in?"

"Yes. *And* I know about how Roscoe Brown got shot in the leg by Parker Simmons in a card game down at the garage because Roscoe Brown called Mrs. Simmons a sack of something."

That stopped him.

"How do you know that?" he asked, squinting up his eyes and using his special x-ray truth vision on me.

"I forget," I muttered, slipping by him into the living room.

He laid his keys and cigarettes and lighter down on the table, and started to unsnap the .38 he kept in a shoulder holster. "Well, Zip, I can't imagine what all you know, but I bet it isn't near as much as what I've *forgotten*. And I'm not going to tell you about Polly's brother because it's too grown-up a story for you, and you should just leave that poor child alone about it. Just in case you're thinking about pestering her."

"I wasn't going to pester her," I said softly, fully intending to. I walked my fingers very slowly and silently toward his gun. I just wanted to give it a little rub.

Dad turned toward the den, and as he walked away he said without looking behind him, "You thinking about touching that gun?"

"No, sir," I said, putting my hand speedy-quick in my pocket.

"That's good." He disappeared behind the curtain that separated the living room from the den. We didn't do any living in the living room—we did it all in the den—but no one seemed to have caught on enough to change the names.

I rode by my brother's house, where he moved after he got married, just in case he had forgotten he didn't read the paper and then accidentally read it. He wasn't home, which was just as well, because he almost never spoke to me. It appeared that he just didn't like anyone and I was no exception. Then I rode over to my sister's house, who always, always spoke to me. She had been married for a year and a half and I was welcome in her house anytime, which I took advantage of, because she had the smallest, sweetest house I'd ever seen. It was very warm and cozy inside, so cozy, in fact, that twice she'd set it on fire. Now every time I rode past it I checked for suspicious smoke, but today appeared to be a good day.

I went in through her kitchen door without knocking. "Lindy! Hey, Lindy! I'm looking for the *Courier-Times*! Did you read it?"

I heard her call from her bedroom, "I'm back here!"

She was sitting at her sewing machine, making curtains for the nursery down the hall. She wasn't pregnant yet, but would be anytime, because nobody would be a better mother, which was a thing God definitely paid attention to when He was passing out babies.

"Hey, you stinkin' little kid," she said without turning around. It was her way of saying love to me. "How was your day at school? Have you seen Dad yet? Is he drinking?"

"What? No, he only drinks at work." My sister could ask the weirdest questions. "My day was fine, thanks," I said fast, nearly waving my hands with impatience. "Hey. Do you know that Polly girl in my class?"

Melinda stopped sewing for a second and looked up. Her back was still to me. "Yes, I do. I baby-sat for her a few times when she was younger. She's an amazingly sweet child, which causes me to suspect that you're not friends with her." She went back to sewing.

"Of course I'm friends with her," I said, sitting down on the floor next to her so I could see her face, in case she decided to start lying. "I mean I like her a lot, or whatever."

"Mmm hmm," she said, and the sewing machine made the same sound. "Why do you ask?" She was already suspicious.

"I was just wondering if maybe you'd read today's paper and maybe there was something in there about Polly's older brother which is a very dramatic story and caused Polly to cry on Mrs. O'Dell this morning."

"Ahh," she said, lifting up the pedal foot and snipping some threads. The curtains were bright yellow, for either a boy or a girl. She'd already painted a big, smiling sun on the wall, by hand. She could do anything. "As a matter of fact, I do know the story you're trying so desperately to hear, and I'm not going to tell you because I imagine Dad has already told you no and the last thing I need is to get in any worse with him. Plus you'd just tell Rose and everyone else you know and cause Polly more pain. So forget it."

"But Lindy! It's already been in the paper! How come I'm the only person alive who's not allowed to know it?" She was making me so mad I was completely dismantling the rubber on my sneakers.

"Because you're too little," she said, looking me in the eye for the first time. She had her beautiful black hair tied back in a ponytail and her gray eyes were so wide and bright she looked like somebody had just made her up out of an idea.

"How can you say that? I'm *so* big."

"Oh, yeah? Tell me one big thing about you."

"Okay, I can ride my bike standing up on the seat."

"That doesn't sound so big to me. That sounds like you in the emergency room, yet again."

"The emergency room isn't so bad. All the nurses are so nice to me."

She harummphed. "Of course they are. They all have crushes on your father."

"He's your father, too." I secretly suspected that Slim Jenkins wasn't actually related to Melinda. In the past month I'd heard Dad accuse Mom of having secret love interests with both Richard Boone and Isaac Asimov.

"Is not."

"Is, too."

"You know what would show me how big you are? If you let this thing with Polly drop and didn't pursue it, if you just left her alone and didn't cause her any grief. That would be a very big thing."

I stood up fast. "I've got to go. I've got some stuff to do. Those are real pretty curtains."

As I walked out the door I heard my sister yell, "Think about it!"

And I yelled back, "I can't hear you!"

By the time I went to bed that night I had encountered four people who knew the story and wouldn't tell me and twice that many who didn't know what I was talking about and couldn't figure out what I was doing at their door. Donnie Fisher thought I was selling something for school with an amazingly convoluted sales pitch, and Agnes Johnson asked me first thing if my mother knew where I was, which stopped me cold, because my mother almost never knew where I was.

"No, ma'am," I answered, involuntarily telling the truth.

"Then go home," she said, shutting her front door.

I WOKE UP the next morning greatly determined to solve the mystery. I marched down to school early, without Rose, and sat at my desk studying a poem I was certain Mrs. Denver didn't know existed. It was called "Preface to a Twenty Volume Suicide Note," by a man named Leroi Jones, and the more I studied it the more it agitated me. When I had read the stanza "And now, each night I count the stars,/And each night I get the same number./And when they will not come to be counted,/I count the holes they leave" for the fifth time, I decided to tear the poem out of the book and throw it away, just to make it gone. At the top of the page, where it met the spine, I made a tiny little tear. The sound it made was awful. I stopped and wiped my hands on my pants, then tried again, but I just couldn't do it. The book was so clean and white, and the letters were so perfectly black and defenseless; it would have been like tearing the ears off a kitten.

I closed the book and put my head down on my desk in order to formulate a plan. I would probably start by just asking all of my classmates if they knew the story. Surely somebody's parents talked about Current Events at the dinner table. Not Kelly's parents, the Hickses; they were the last people in the world to carry tales. And not the Newmans—nobody ever said anything in that house but me. Rose's parents were too sophisticated to care; Dana's parents had undoubtedly spent the evening chain-smoking and bowling in New Castle. Rachel's parents only talked about Jesus; Sammy and Smarty didn't have a dinner table; Jackie didn't have parents. If I asked Mrs. O'Dell she'd just smack me and make me sad, and Mrs. Denver had such a bug-eyed innocence I didn't dare ask her for fear she'd betray herself. That left only one person: Polly herself.

I decided to approach the situation in a straightforward way. I wrote her a note: "Dear Polly, Please meet me back here during recess. I need to ask you something." I had just finished folding it when Mrs. O'Dell came shuffling in, carrying her old blue book bag.

"Hey, Mrs. O'Dell," I said, giving her a little wave.

"Causing trouble, are you?" she said, trying to focus on me.

"No! Why would you say that?"

"Because I've known you your whole life, that's why." She sat down at her desk in the corner and started to adjust the papers she had to grade. Her glasses were about an inch thick, and were something like quatrafocals, so she had to bob her head up and down to keep things in focus.

When the other students began arriving, I noticed that Mrs. O'Dell wasn't harsh with any of them. In fact, all adults were harder on me than anybody else. My teachers generally didn't like me, and considered me to be the source of any disruption, even when I was perfectly (or basically) innocent; Edythe wanted to kill me; Doc Holiday yelled at me every time I walked in the drugstore, even though I was such a faithful customer; Rose's parents considered me pure trouble. A person could easily work herself into a state by pondering such things. Luckily, Polly came in and distracted me.

I walked over to the coat rack like I was going to get something out of my jacket pocket, and dropped the note on her desk as I passed by. She was very surprised, and did not handle the transaction with any finesse. She stared at me hard for about half a minute, then looked at the note. As I passed her on my way back to my desk she said, "Did you drop this?"

"No! Read it!"

Mrs. O'Dell was trying desperately to see who was talking, but we were just out of range. When I dared look back at Polly a few minutes later she just nodded at me, wide-eyed.

When I snuck back in our classroom during recess Polly was already sitting quietly at her desk. I chose the chair in front of her, straddling it backward.

"You know about my brother, don't you?" she asked, tears filling her eyes. Her face was bigger than those of other girls our age. She was heavier and more developed. I could see that there were a number of things separating her from the rest of us.

"Well," I began, trying to be at least a little bit honest. "I know *something*. I really just wanted to hear about it from you. I didn't want to believe the wrong thing."

And then she started wailing in earnest. She didn't try to wipe her face or control it or anything. If I'd ever seen Julie crying like this, she would have assassinated me.

"He didn't mean to kill that man!" she wailed, which I knew from Perry Mason was a miserable way to begin a defense.

"Whoa, whoa. Why don't you just start at the beginning and tell me the whole story." I sounded oddly adult and comforting, even to myself, which was when I knew that I was genuinely a bad person, and that was why adults treated me the way they did. But Polly bought it completely, and started at the beginning.

Her brother had been an officer in the Marines, and a prisoner of war. It had taken a long time for him to get home, but a few months ago he had arrived back in Indiana. He was anxious to see his wife, but when he went to their small, rented farmhouse, she no longer lived there. When he pressed her parents, who were elderly and frightened, they told him that she was living in a mobile home with an old drinking buddy of his whose name, ironically, was Butcher.

He went to Butcher's trailer with a loaded .12 gauge shotgun, a detail that would be important in his trial. When his former friend opened the door, Polly's brother shot him once in the chest, then turned around and went home to his parents. He confessed all of it, blandly, to the police.

As if this weren't bad enough, the prosecution had in its possession a photograph that Polly's family was desperate to keep out of the trial. The judge had already ruled it admissible, so they had no hope that it wouldn't be used as evidence. It showed Polly's brother in a village in Vietnam whose name I had never heard before, but which would be heard many times in the years to come. He was standing atop an enormous pile of dead civilians, including women and infants, with his rifle in the air, bellowing. His hair had turned snow white.

Polly cried and cried. She loved her brother the way I loved my sister, even loved the stranger who had come home in his place. She cried not because he might go to jail for the rest of his life, but because she didn't want people to think ill of him, and even more, she wanted it to never have happened. She wanted to undo it all.

It wasn't until she finished her story that I realized how hard my heart was pounding, and how much I just wanted to get up and leave the room. Even without extensive tact conditioning, I realized I was stuck in the situation I had created, a situation in which a girl was sobbing out a story I had no business demanding.

I went to Mrs. O'Dell's desk and brought Polly a box of Kleenex. Old women always know the value of tissues. She was just wiping her face and blowing her nose when Mrs. Denver came in to find us.

"Hey, girls! Come on out to the playground and join us. No use sitting in here moping." Mrs. Denver could be crazily cheerful.

I looked at my teacher and realized that she thought I had taken Polly under my wing. She thought I was trying to help her, which was the last thing in the world I wanted to do. I suddenly felt very, very busy. I had so many things going on. All my life I had heard that you can't help everyone, and Polly, quite obviously, was everyone.

Mrs. Denver took Polly by the hand and led her outside. I walked a few steps behind them. Mrs. Denver's entrance had prevented me from having to respond to Polly's story in any way, which was a miracle of luck. I watched the two of them head toward the open field where kids were gathered in clusters, playing games, Mrs. Denver scuttling in her nervous, good-willed way, Polly already taller than the adult walking next to her, and cumbersome.

I sat down on the steps of the fourth-grade shack. I had never heard, never imagined a story that featured a mountain of dead women and children. I had never heard of a man's hair going white from violence and shock.

I crossed my arms over my knees and rested my head on them. Ants scurried back and forth across the sidewalk in what appeared to be a prescribed route. I had yet to hear a satisfactory explanation about why ants carried their dead right back into the ant village and down the ant hole, but that's what some of them were doing as I watched. My mom had suggested to me that if I didn't know the scientific answer for something, I should choose the most obvious explanation. And the obvious explanation for why the ants hauled their dead back home was, clearly, compassion.

Halfway across the field Polly had stopped and turned back toward me. She was standing perfectly still, and when I looked up at her she waved, tentatively. I waved back, sighed, and began to make my way toward her.

ARISEN

My mom and I were in my parents' bedroom, discussing what I would wear to the Easter sunrise service at church.

"I'm not going."

"Yes. You are. We have this problem every year, and every year you have to go, and yes, you are going to wear a dress," my mom said patiently.

"I'm not going and I'm not wearing a dress."

Mom didn't answer. She just maddeningly

continued flipping through old dress patterns, trying to find one that might cause the least amount of rioting.

"Mother, do you know why it's called 'sunrise service'?"

"I think I do."

"Because it's held at sunrise. Now, I just can't be expected to get up at that time, unless I'm going fishing."

She put down the pattern she was studying and looked at me over the top of her glasses. "This is a thing that troubles me," she began. "You are perfectly willing to get up in the dead of night to go fishing with your father, but I have to fight you to get you to do it once a year, *one time a year*, with me."

I threw myself face down on her bed and began kicking my feet so hard her bedspread flew up in the air and covered me. Mom was all the time using unfair arguments, and sometimes I could figure out where she had cheated and sometimes a reply just escaped me. This time, though, I got her.

"Aha!" I said, sitting up quickly. "I have to go to church with you three times a week! That's something like six thousand times a year. How many times do I get to go fishing with Dad?"

"That's beside the point." She was terse, and turned back to the patterns and the sewing machine.

"Also," I said, unable to control the momentum of how right I was, "it's freezing cold outside on Easter Sunday and every year I just stand there with my teeth clacking, and singing outside *in a dress* in the freezing cold is the most stupidest thing I can think of."

"You can't say 'most stupidest.' Stupidest is not a word, and even if it were, it implies most."

"And also I don't even like Easter. It's the stupidest of all the holidays. What kind of a retard would believe in a giant bunny who happens to not even come to my house. Can you explain that, please?"

"Which part?" she said, looking back at me.

"Why the Easter Bunny doesn't come to my house."

"Because Easter is a religious holiday. I don't believe in the candy part of it."

"Well, that's a fine thing! You should see the baskets the Easter Bunny leaves at Rose's house! Which he does because William and Joyce believe in the candy part! Rose and Maggie get enough candy for the rest of the year, plus sometimes one of those little soap lambs they like to eat."

Mom had apparently found the pattern she was looking for, because she was studying it in a pleased way which flat-out caused my stomach to sink.

"Look at this one, sweetie," she said, holding it out for me. "I could make it out of blue-and-white gingham, and it's got this little collar that I could embroider flowers on. It will be perfect for spring."

I turned my head, put my hands over my ears and began humming "Twinkle, Twinkle." I was trying to be very clear about seeing and hearing no evil.

I felt her gently removing my hands from my head. "Listen to me," she said, turning my head to face her. "Easter is about Jesus rising up into Heaven after he was crucified. It's about how he still lives with and for us."

"Mom," I said, for what must have been the eighty-fourth time. "How can you believe such a thing?!"

She put her hands in her lap and sighed. "Because I have to, angel. I don't have any choice."

I stood up and looked at her for a second. My mom was nothing but a mystery sometimes. As I reached for the door I said, "Well, I don't have to believe it." And she let me go with the last word.

IN ADDITION TO ALL the humiliations I was heir to, when Mom made me a dress that I would have rather eaten hominy than wear, I was forced to try it on while it still had pins in it. Whoever thought of such a thing? In a normal world, if I had said to my mom that I was just going to slip on these jeans and this T-shirt, which P.S. were full of straight pins, she would have felt my head for a fever. I had to stand on a three-legged milking stool for the punishment, too, which was none too steady but the perfect height for measuring a hem. Sometimes my sister was there to assist, and she was not against me getting stuck by a pin. In fact, she was always delighted by the prospect of me in a dress.

"Are you going to make her brush her teeth, too?" Melinda asked, gleefully.

"No," I answered, crossing my arms over my chest.

"Yes," Mom said, around the pins she had between her teeth.

"Maybe we could pull her hair back in two little barrettes, like this. Oh, no, wait, that just makes her wings more noticeable. Hmmm. Maybe we could pull all of her hair up on top of her head and slick it into a little curl with some Vaseline, like you used to do when she was a baby." She had her hands all in my hair, making me kind of sleepy and mad.

"Lindy, don't pick," Mom said, but she was distracted.

"I know! A hat! She can wear a little Easter bonnet, like I used to. Have you ever had an Easter bonnet?" she asked, tilting her head in a quizzical way, as if she didn't know that I'd poke out my own eye before I'd wear anything except a proper knit cap on my head.

"And if you're worried about your legs getting cold, let me suggest some nice, fuzzy tights, the kind that don't go all the way to your crotch, but stop just in the middle of your thigh."

I swung out at her, but she ducked.

"Girls!" my mom said, dropping two or three pins out of her exasperated mouth, which I would find later with my bare feet.

I narrowed up my eyes at my sister in a furious way. "Is there a reason you torture me so much?"

"Yes, as a matter of fact, yes, there is. But I can't tell you. It's a secret." And she straightened up the hem of the dress just a little and managed to poke me fourteen times.

"Mom, I'm counting to five and then I'm getting down off this stool."

She didn't even look at me. "You'll get down when I'm done, sweetheart, and not before. Now straighten up."

I straightened up. At the very end of the ordeal they fastened the little collar around my neck, which was just a fraction too tight. It was, in fact, made of blue-and-white gingham, and my mother had, as she threatened, embroidered a variety of pastel flowers on the collar. In order not to choke on it I counted in my head: only one, two, three, four, five, six, seven, eight, nine more years until I could leave home. Eighteen was the age that Julie and I planned to both buy our own farm and hit the open road, in no particular order.

MOM SHOOK MY SHOULDER GENTLY. I burrowed more deeply into my sleeping bag, until all that was sticking out was my hair sprouts. As soon as I had my face inside my sleeping bag, I knew for certain how desperately I didn't want to leave it. It was incredibly warm, and there is simply nothing more comforting than the smell of one's own bed. I was wearing my favorite flannel pajamas, too, which kind of stuck to the inside of my sleeping bag like Jesus and the Apostles on the flannel-board at church. The pajamas were bright yellow, with brown cowboys and lassos. I refused to give them up, even though the pant legs stopped just below my knees. Besides having my hair problem and my face problem and teeth too big, and besides being always the tallest, skinniest girl in my class, I had what my sister called "the unfortunate situation" of being deformed. Most clothes that we bought in a store came in sets, and if the shirt fit me even reasonably well, the pants were too short. We had tried buying the sets with the pants the right length, which meant my mom had to take in the waist, and the shirt fell right off my shoulders. I was thinking maybe the solution would be to find the girl who was deformed exactly the opposite of me, and we could share.

"You've got to get up now," my mom was saying, as if she was in her right mind.

"Mom!" I sat up angrily. "It must be four-thirty in the morning! What are you doing waking me up?!"

"It's exactly four-thirty in the morning," she said, happily bustling around the den. I could see that she had laid out the dreaded Easter dress on the couch like a shroud.

Dad was sitting in his chair with his arms crossed. When I met his eye he just shrugged one shoulder, as if to say he was entirely helpless in what was about to happen to me.

I grumbled out of bed and stood shivering next to the coal stove. I was instantly cold in the way that causes the spine to shrink up. In desperation, I put my forehead against the black enamel stove and burned it, just a little. Then I tried to straighten up, but failed. I scrunched over again, put my forehead against the stove, and burned it. After I did it the third time I had no choice but to look at my father.

"You want to just open the door and stick your head inside?" he said, with his arms still crossed.

"Daddy. Are you going to get me out of this, yes or no."

"No."

I headed for the bathroom, which turned out to be much warmer than the den, because Dad had gone in and turned on the heater, well before Mom woke me up. I sat on the floor in front of it, scrunched up into a ball. I heard my mom call from the den.

"What are you doing in there?"

"Brushing my teeth!" I shouted, under the door.

"Why isn't the water running?"

I jumped up and turned the water on, then quick opened the medicine cabinet and jostled the toothpaste around noisily. Unable to think of any more delays, I walked back into the den miserably.

"Okay," I said, holding my arms up in surrender. "Put the dress on me."

But because it was so cold outside I had to first put on a scratchy undershirt, and then a slip that I would have sworn hadn't fit me two years ago, and then the fuzzy tights that stopped in the middle of my thighs, and *then* the dress. By the time I picked up my little pink New Testament and said good-bye to my dad, I also had on snow boots, a scarf, my gloves, and my winter coat with the hood up and tied.

Mom and I trudged the one block down the street. It was still dark, but I could see a little light on the horizon. We would gather in the meadow behind the church, which happened to face the east, so we would see the sunrise in its glory. There were three churches in Mooreland, and they all had sunrise services, but we were the only ones with a meadow, which was, really, no kind of claim if you didn't want to be there in the first place.

Pastor Eddie and his wife, Shirley, were standing in the meeting place. There would be no more than fifteen or twenty of us, because common sense can prevail even with the most faithful. Shirley had brought two baskets of lilies, which looked especially beautiful on the still winter ground, and I could see that under their coats, everyone was dressed in their best clothes. The Hicks family were all there, making up more than half the assembled number, and so there was the sweetness and festivity that they took everywhere with them. There is a kind of wildness that grows up among people who have gathered in the dark, and we all felt a little giddy.

After we had stood in silence for just a few cold minutes, Pastor Eddie raised his head and said, "I'm so glad to see you all here today."

And a few of the grown-ups who had no self-control, including my mother, said amen.

He told us that there was no greater day of celebration anywhere on the calendar, not even Christmas, because this was the day that Jesus truly revealed himself as Lord, by throwing off the shackles of death that no other human being had ever escaped. Then he asked us to go backward in the story a little bit, and think about those days that Jesus spent on the cross, and how his mother must have felt watching him die so slowly. How she spent every waking hour at the foot of the cross, offering him comfort, as we must do now, in our hearts. And how, at the very moment of his death, the whole world, indeed, the entire universe, was simply silent. And we all stood silent.

I felt, suddenly, wide awake. The sun was just coming up over the horizon, and I looked at the faces of the Friends gathered around me. Some had closed their eyes; some, like my mother, were looking at the sky. At the fence bordering our meadow and a neighboring farmer's field, a small group of horses had gathered, and were standing perfectly still and watching us. Their breath steamed out in the cold. Down the street the bells of the North Christian Church began to ring, and it was morning.

Eddie finished the story of Jesus's death, and how he was carried to the tomb, and the rolled stone, and his appearance to the five thousand, and then we stood in a circle and sang "Christ Arose," "He Lives," and "I Serve a Risen Savior."

I looked up at my mother as her voice rang out above all the others. She had made an Easter dress for me, but not one for herself. She was wearing an old gray dress Mom Mary had given her, out of season, and a red plaid coat that looked like a horse blanket, with buttons. She looked down and saw me staring at her, and took her gloveless hand out of her coat and rested it on my head. I leaned up against her and put my hand in her warm pocket, where she always kept some Kleenex and those Vick's cough drops that taste brown.

Every year I forgot how short the sunrise service really was; how quickly we were inside the church for coffee and sweet rolls. We would even get to go home for a few hours, then come back for the regular Easter service, the one the normal people attended, including my rotten sister, who with her husband slept right through the sunrise on Jesus's high holiday.

On the way home, Mom stopped me just as we reached Reed and Mary Ball's house.

"Look! Do you see those flowers? Those are called crocus. Aren't they beautiful?"

I couldn't think of what to say. I'd seen the crocus every year of my life, and they always just looked like fierce little weeds to me. "They sure are purple," I managed, which caused Mom to nod her head as if that were the whole point of them.

In the afternoon of that day, after she had helped me out of my dress and my tights, Mom walked me down to William and Joyce's, where the Easter Bunny had come, and Rose and Maggie met me at the door with their brimming baskets of eggs and chocolates and soap, and just like every year before, they told me to take as much as I wanted—they had more than they could ever finish.

THE SOCIAL GOSPEL

Ibriefly took up with a little Holiness convert girl named Sissy Bellings. One of Sissy's front teeth always pointed north, and every day she wore one of her dead Granny's dresses, which drooped where her Granny used to keep her bosoms, and hung unevenly to the floor. Sissy's dun-colored braid reached the small of her back, and little wisps of hair slipped free and framed her face. I found Sissy very exotic, not just for the tooth and the dresses, but because of the way she always sat alone with a Holiness look on her face.

Sissy was the half sister (or maybe the whole sister, no one knew for sure) of Sammy Bellings, a mean little girl with a flat face I was quite fond of. We were all in the same grade. Sissy and Sammy and their fifteen siblings lived together in a two-room house next to the diner, and not one of them was anything like the other. There were babies of them, and one girl old enough to have babies of her own. One high school boy called Trick was so pretty he looked like an angel on a postcard, only with a good tan and big muscles. There was a retarded boy who spent all his life riding a tiny bicycle, and another boy, also with scant resources in the brain region, who loved rock'n'roll and refused to bathe. We called him Smarty. He was in the fourth grade for the fourth time. Smarty drove our poor teacher, Mrs. Denver, to bitter distraction. One spring afternoon when it came time for recess, Smarty asked Mrs. Denver if he could stay inside with her for the fifth day in a row. Exasperated, Mrs. Denver stood up and shouted, "Oh, good Lord! Why don't you just go outside and blow some stink off!" We all laughed so hard that the little epileptic boy peed in his pants and Mrs. Denver started to cry.

Befriending Sissy was not much of a challenge. All I had to do was sit with her at lunch one day, back in the corner where she always sat alone reading her Bible, which had also belonged to Granny, and had a Granny's Bible look: a cracked black leather cover with the words *Holy Bible* in flaking silver letters. The paper was so thin the letters of one page showed up through another, and when the book was closed the pages formed a solid band of gold so delicate and beautiful it would have made a pirate weep.

I sat down next to Sissy. We were eating exactly the same lunch, for which I had paid fifteen cents and Sissy got for free: chicken and noodles, smooshy peas, rice with brown sugar, white bread and butter, and a carton of milk. She looked up at me questioningly. We'd gone to school together from the beginning and never dined together. I tried not to stare at her tooth, but it drew my gaze against my will.

"Sissy, I want to be a better Christian," which was a terrible lie, but just for a moment, as I said it, I believed it.

"Ain't you a Friend?" she asked. I wanted to see what the relationship would be between her tooth and that bread and butter.

"Yep. My whole life."

"Then why ain't you a good Christian?"

"I don't know. I never get the fruits of the spirit. I don't go to altar call. I don't think I love the grown-up Jesus enough."

Sissy pondered my confession with a Holy look, but didn't pick up her bread.

"Don't let me interrupt your lunch," I said, solicitously.

"This is important." Sissy pushed her tray away. "Do you do good works?"

"Excuse me?"

"Good works. Do you do a good deed every day?"

I thought about it. The only good deeds I performed were acts of self-denial. Earlier that week, for instance, I had stuffed all my schoolbooks in the big trash barrel destined for the incinerator, and then gotten them back out when I realized Tony the janitor had seen me. Tony wasn't a bit afraid of pointing a finger.

"Maybe not quite every day."

"Pastor says we have to do good and be good because His eye is on the sparrow."

"Your pastor's eye is on a sparrow?" I couldn't imagine what the people of Sissy's church looked like, all gathered up together.

"God. God's eye."

"What kind of good deeds? Like Girl Scouts? Because I got kicked out of Brownies and they won't give me another chance to keep my clothes on at camp. Also all we ever learned was housework. I'm not much for it."

"I don't think you have to be in Girl Scouts to do good." Sissy sat very still, with her hands gathered up humbly in her lap. Children were screaming and spitting milk all around us, but I felt like I was in the quietest place in the world, watching her. "And housework doesn't count unless you do it because your mama will have a breakdown and move back to Kentucky without you if you don't."

I tapped on the table with my fingertips and absent-mindedly began picking at my lunch. "Are you allowed to tell me some? Or do I just have to stand around waiting for one to need me?"

Sissy leaned close to me. Her tooth arrived first. "You have to pray about it. Just ask the Lord and He will hear thee and he will put it in your heart to be good. Do you want to pray with me right now?"

"No, thanks." I picked up my fork and dug into my chicken and noodles, then skedaddled out of the lunchroom as fast as I could.

IN THE FOURTH GRADE, we were allowed to start studying band instruments with a local man who could play or repair anything that made music. His name was Mr. Sewell, and he drove across town to our school once a week in a station wagon loaded down with clarinets and flutes and trumpets. Mrs. Denver asked all interested children to stay after school one day to talk to him. There were about six of us, and Mr. Sewell went around the circle and asked us what instrument we were interested in playing. Rose wanted to play a flute. He nodded. Margaret wanted to play a trumpet. That was good. Brian really wanted to play a tuba, but would settle for a saxophone. Mr. Sewell looked relieved. Roger, the epileptic boy, had always dreamed of playing the clarinet. Sandy, who was much older than the rest of us and appeared not to have any vocal cords, refused to answer. Mr. Sewell looked at me.

"I'd like to play the drums."

Mr. Sewell smiled, but shook his head. "Girls don't play drums. How about a piccolo?"

"I'd rather play the drums."

"What about a French horn?"

"What about the drums?"

The other kids started to squirm and Rose kicked me lightly under my chair. Mr. Sewell had a look on his face I didn't like, and I suddenly noticed how big he was, and how he had a mustache, and black bristly hairs growing off the tops of his fingers.

He said, with exaggerated patience, "I'll let you play a percussion instrument, like the bells or xylophone, but not drums. This is your last chance."

"Okay. I'll play the bells." By this time all I cared about was making him load in that station wagon the heaviest instrument available to me, and I imagined that a set of bells was pretty dog-gone heavy.

I SPENT EVERY AFTERNOON stalking good works. My first victim was Agnes Johnson who was 164 years old. Her skin, impatient for her to get it over with and die, appeared to be sliding down off her body into a pool around her ankles. She was older than dirt, but feisty. She insisted on cutting her own grass every week with an ancient push mower. For years I'd seen her out there, pushing against the mower as if it were a huge rock, her skinny arms quivering, her lips trembling, a thin film of sweat shining on the place most people had an upper lip. I'd never paid her much mind, but on this particular day I realized I'd hit the jackpot. Ordinarily I'd have rather run naked into a rose bush than cut grass; at my own house I suggested a few times a week that we get a goat or some other furry grazing thing to live in the backyard. (I thought a goat was an especially clever choice because they could also eat our empty tin cans.) So if I mowed Agnes Johnson's yard, I could probably avoid doing any more good deeds until I myself was flat-out old.

When I reached Agnes's house I jumped off my bike while it was still moving. It rolled on a few feet like a headless chicken, then crashed into the hedge at the edge of Agnes's yard.

Her back was to me. I ran up next to her, but she was concentrating so intently on making the mower move that she didn't see me. The blades made a quiet snickety snickety snickety sound. Agnes was moving maybe an eighth of an inch an hour—her grass was not so much getting cut as dying from natural causes. In the center of her side yard was a little round flower garden surrounded by stones Agnes had painted white. She was headed straight for it. I figured if I assumed the helm and just cut the grass around the flower bed, that would be enough. I could tell Sissy the next day that I *was* good and I'd *done* good, and then I could sit with her at lunch every day and eventually be invited over to her house where

I could get a good long look at whatever went on in those two rooms.

"Hey, Agnes," I said, since it appeared she was never going to notice me. She didn't turn around. I reached out and touched her on the arm. "Hey, Agnes." She kept pushing the mower. I called her name one more time, then decided I'd just insinuate myself onto the handles of the mower. I put my right hand next to Agnes's left hand and gradually started scooting it over. Her grip was surprisingly fierce. I heard her breath stutter, and a little whistle in the back of her throat. She was positively free of lips. I hopscotched over her left hand and gripped the mower handle in the middle, then grasped the edge with my left hand and began pushing Agnes to the side with my hip.

I was almost home free—I had scooted her nearly completely away from the mower when she noticed me. She turned her head slowly; her eyes stopped on every object in the arc between her face and mine.

"Get away!" she shouted, spit flying. I noticed she was wearing a nightgown and old houseslippers covered with little grass carcasses.

"Agnes, I've come to good-deed you. Let me cut the rest of your yard." I was pulling on the mower and so was she, and she was winning.

"Shoo! Get away, pesty girl!"

"Agnes! It's me, the little Jarvis! You taught my brother in the third grade and told him he was stupid, don't you know me?"

"Let go of my property, villain! I'll call the Law!"

"I've come to help you!"

"This is how I take the air," she said, shoving me away with her own hip, which I suddenly feared would snap like a dry twig.

I let go of the mower and stepped away, winded. Agnes was a tough nut. She centered herself and leaned into her task. The blades whispered, and stray grasses flew out the sides and stuck to my bare feet.

ONCE A WEEK after school Mr. Sewell came to the fourth-grade building with my orchestra bells, which were in a coffin-shaped box I could barely lift. I played the metal bells with metal mallets. Rose's silver flute, by comparison, was just a sweet, breathy surprise, and every time I struck a note (at the beginning of every measure) I thought I saw her wince.

Playing the bells or the xylophone was essentially playing a piano with sticks, so there wasn't much for me to do and not much for Mr. Sewell to teach me. Those instruments that required blowing were a whole different story. It seemed that my classmates would never catch on to how to make a real note come out. A couple of them simply could not pucker and move their fingers at the same time, no matter how patient Mr. Sewell was.

Rose, though, showed promise. Mr. Sewell asked if she'd like to start staying for an hour after band practice to work on scales and she said yes. Rose wanted to do everything well. I wanted to do everything quickly. On the first day she was scheduled to stay, as soon as practice was over I slid the bells off my lap and onto the floor so fast they clanged, then I dropped my mallets on top and went flying out the door. Mr. Sewell yelled, "Come back in here and take care of your . . ." I yelled behind me, "I can't hear you!" And kept running.

I ran all the way to Sissy's house, which was a long way, just over a block. The house was squashed between an abandoned building that had once been a grocery store, and the diner, which had once been a house. An onion-ring smell billowed out of the diner perpetually. I couldn't imagine how Sissy and her brothers and sisters endured it all day—it made me ravenous. Just standing there for thirty seconds contemplating Sissy's front door and I was chewing on my thumb.

It was a shotgun house, covered with brown, speckled, asbestos shingles, some of which looked like they'd been gnawed. Nothing grew in the few feet of dirt on either side of the front step, but shards of broken bottles sparkled like treasure. I walked up the two cement steps and faced the door. I turned the rusty knob of the screen door, which was just a frame without a trace of a screen, then raised my fist to knock on the splintering storm door. Before I could, Sissy opened it. She didn't look the least surprised to see me.

An amazing smell waved out around her, a terrifying human smell of diapers and food and old furniture and tooth decay. I had just enough time to pop my head around her before she slipped out and closed the door. The front room was almost completely dark, although the day was brilliant. A black-and-white television flickered on a dozen faces, who seemed to occupy every available space, languidly.

Sissy was beside me so quick and quiet she spooked me. Her dress for that day was black with little sprigs of some no-color flower. The bosom parts were down around her waist. She was carrying her Bible, and I noticed for the first time how little her hands were, and how the nails were chewed down to nothing. I wanted, for just a second, to step inside her skin, to know the feeling of carrying a Bible the way she carried it, like a shield or like a baby. I wanted to sleep in a big bed with six sisters whose smell I recognized, and to be different from them, because I was Holy. I wanted to have only one choice and no other, the way she had chosen the dresses and the covenant. And at the same time I wanted to have already done it and be back at my own house, which suddenly looked perfectly reasonable by comparison.

"Have you done your good works yet?" Sissy looked up at me, blinking in the afternoon light.

"Almost. I started to. I about did. No."

She leaned in close to me, the way she had in the lunch room. Her voice was just above a whisper. "You must stick fast unto the Lord. It is not easy, but His will be done. There will be stones in your path, sin and temptings. Just love the Lord your God with all of your heart and He will show the way, the truth and the life. I have to cook dinner." She opened the door and slipped back inside before I could say a word. I tried peeking through a window to see the flickering television, but the outside of the window was covered with plastic and the inside with an old sheet. It might as well have been the middle of the night, in that house.

MOM ASKED ME would I please take two cookie sheets over to my brother's house. His sweet wife, Elaine, needed to borrow them. I threw my arms up in the air in a gesture of *oh, thank goodness, thank goodness.* My good works had come. And they would be easy. And there would eventually be cookies involved.

Mom had stacked the pans on top of each other, but I separated them. I climbed on top of my bike, and with a pan in each hand, pushed off from the little cement wall that surrounded our front yard. She watched me from the front porch.

"Don't you think you should use at least one hand to steer?" she asked.

"Pshaw. I can ride this bike all over town with no hands."

Mom kindly refrained from mentioning my many, many visits to the emergency room. She also kindly refrained mentioning the little incident last summer which had resulted in my losing two toe-nails, severely abrading the top of my foot, and breaking two toes. At the hospital the nurse had asked how I'd done it, and I had to admit that the injuries were because of my foot being run over while it was upside-down, by a bicycle *I myself was riding.* The nurse clapped, and then went and got all the other nurses who were familiar with me, and they all applauded, too.

I rested the pans on my open palms the way a waiter might carry plates of spaghetti to the Mafia. When I got to the stop sign at Charles and Broad I slowed down just long enough to look for cars, but of course there weren't any. I rode past the Newmans' little car wash, and then the house on the corner, and turned. I was doing great. All I had to do was ride straight down this street for a long time, almost two blocks, and then I'd be there.

I suddenly remembered the railroad tracks, and sped up. Some of my best rodeo tricks with Julie had occurred on this very street, because there was a dip just before the tracks, then an immediate hill. If we hit it going fast enough, our bicycles reared up just like vicious stallions. Ever since Dad straightened out the frame, my bike could go straight ahead for miles without me touching the handle bars.

I sped up some more. I was fifty, thirty, ten feet from the dip, then I hit it, and the last sounds I heard were my head hitting the street, my teeth slamming against each other, and the pans falling on the tracks with an angry clatter. I saw a bright light and thought, *Don't walk toward it, even if dead people you once loved waggle their fingers invitingly!* The light receded, and I saw stars, like in a cartoon. I heard two strange sounds, and gradually made out what they were: the first was a pitiful wheezing coming from my own chest, which signaled the collapse of one of my lungs, and the other was a siren. I was just coherent enough to wonder how it was possible, given that I was ten miles from the nearest hospital, that an ambulance had arrived so soon.

The ambulance skidded to a stop beside me, and the driver jumped off. It was Sissy's older retarded brother, Levon, on his tiny bicycle. His aaaaah-oooooooh sounds dwindled down to a whine. He hadn't spoken English in about fifteen years, so I didn't even try to talk to him. I just let him loop his arms under my armpits and heave me up to my feet. My vision was still swimming. Levon silently brushed the gravel off my back, wiped away the blood that was running down my chin, gathered up the pans, rolled my unscathed bicycle back to me, then climbed on his own bike and pedaled away.

"For Pete's sake," I muttered, watching Levon speed down the street. Even his old white shirt cresting out behind him looked heroic. I trudged the rest of the way to Dan and Elaine's house dejectedly, and handed the pans to Elaine without a word. When I got home I climbed up into the hollow of my favorite tree and lay looking at the sky. It seemed there were some things about myself I was going to have to face. I thought about them while I picked out the sharp pieces of gravel still embedded in the heel of my foot.

WHEN I SPENT THE NIGHT at Rose's house, which was often, we all slept together in the bed Rose and Maggie shared. Before we went to sleep we almost always played a game called Tickle. Tickle was a noncompetitive game, in which the object was to run your fingers up and down the back of the person lying next to you, through her flannel nightgown. I often ended up in the middle, which was good and bad, because it meant that I always got Tickled, but I also never got to stop Tickling. The people on the ends got at least one shift of just lying still and enjoying it.

I was Tickling Maggie's back and Rose was Tickling mine. We were mostly not talking, and it seemed that Maggie was nearly asleep, when Rose scooted over closer to me and whispered, "I'm scared of something."

I whispered back, "What?"

"I don't want to do private lessons with Mr. Sewell anymore."

This didn't surprise me, because I never would have wanted to do it in the first place. "Why? Is it boring and stupid and you'd rather be outside?"

"No." Rose didn't say anything for a long time. "I told my mom, but she thinks I'm making it up or being silly."

"Making what up?"

"I'm just afraid. He . . . never mind. Forget it. It's time to switch." She turned over and I turned over but Maggie just stayed where she was.

Rose didn't say anything more and I didn't ask any questions. I had no idea what she was talking about, but the more I thought about it, the more it worried me. I pictured Mr. Sewell bending over the back of his station wagon, unloading our instruments; the way his light-blue pants stretched tight across his legs; the black hair on his knuckles. He had an enormous smile. And then I saw Rose sitting up so perfectly straight the way she did, her head tilted in a left-handed way, holding her silver flute. She was always so clean that light seemed to catch her everywhere. It glanced off her cheekbones and off her black hair, it lit up her green eyes. Even her flat, square fingernails shone. Whatever was scaring her scared me, too. I Tickled her back a little extra, until I heard her give up and fall asleep. I was awake a long time.

THE NEXT WEEK at band practice everything was perfectly normal: there was tooting and spitting, and when Mr. Sewell asked Sandy to play an A she started crying, which she'd also done the week before. Finally, he puffed out his cheeks and blew out a long sigh and said we could go.

The other kids dried off and unscrewed their instruments, placing them lovingly in the velvet-lined cases, but I didn't move. Rose didn't look at me and I didn't look at her; instead, I concentrated on the piece of music in front of me, which was "Mary Had a Little Lamb." I studied it as if there were movements I couldn't figure out how to interpret. Mr. Sewell came back from loading the station wagon and saw me sitting there.

"You may go, Miss Jarvis. I'm sure you've noticed that the weather is good."

"I need private lessons," I said, without meeting his eye.

"What on earth for? If you want to learn to play a scale all you have to do is hit the keys in the order they're laid out. You already know that."

"I just want private lessons, is all."

He looked at me a moment, then crossed his arms. "There's no reason for you to be here, and you'll disturb Rose, who is serious about playing the flute. My time is limited."

"I'm really serious, too. Also my time is limited. I want to be a better bell player. I've decided it's what I want to do when I grow up."

Mr. Sewell continued to stare at me for quite a while, given how limited his time was. I snuck a glance at Rose, who was looking at her lap. Her cheeks were flushed.

"All right," he finally said. "I'll work with you first and then you can go."

"No, thanks. Actually, I'm supposed to always every single day walk Rose home from school or else. We walk to school together and we walk home together, and if we don't our parents do bad, bad things to us."

"That hasn't seemed to stop you any Wednesday for the past month," he said, with a feigned patience I sometimes heard in my sister's voice when she was getting ready to get wicked.

"Well, I can't take any more punishments. I've taken all I can, and now I just have to do what I'm told and wait for Rose. In fact, you don't even have to private lesson me. I'll just sit over here in the corner and look at a book."

I slid the bells off my lap and they crashed to the floor. I carefully put my mallets in the back of the box, then closed the lid and fastened it. Rose didn't say anything and neither did Mr. Sewell, and when I got to the bookshelf I heard him sigh and say, "Okay, let's start where we left off last week."

When the hour was up Rose cleaned her flute and began putting it away. I helped Mr. Sewell carry my bells out to the car. He offered us a ride, but we turned it down, even though we had a long, long walk ahead of us.

IN THE LUNCHROOM I slipped into the seat next to Sissy. Her hamburger, fried potatoes, creamed corn, and cling peaches sat untouched. She was carefully reading Paul's letter to the Galatians, which was another yawner, as far as I was concerned.

She looked up at me, her eyes bright. Sometimes she chewed on her hair, which made me queasy. Today, fortunately, all of her hair was in her braid.

"Have you done it?" she asked anxiously. I could tell she was afraid I was one who might never be saved.

"Sissy, honestly. Sheesh. You know, no. I can't. Good works just aren't for me. Also I can't pray and I can't go to the altar and I can't say out loud that Jesus is my Lord and Savior and I can't cry in church."

She nodded. It occurred to me that she had seen into my heart from the beginning. She looked at her lap for a moment, then said, "Knock and the door shall be opened; ask and ye shall receive. It is never too late for the humble and broken in spirit." She looked back at Galatians with a kind of finality.

I sat there for a few more minutes, testing out my lunch. I was almost constantly hungry. Sissy would never take me in her house, and while she would always be nice to me, just the way she had been nice to me through my recent failures, there was something about her that couldn't be touched. For the rest of that year, when I saw her on the playground or passed her on the sidewalk, she would smile at me with her enormous tooth and then go on about her business, which was God's business, and had nothing to do with me.

THE LETTER

There never was a town more beautiful at Christmas than Mooreland, Indiana. We didn't hang decorations on every telephone pole, the way some towns do, and we didn't have a community Christmas tree. Instead, Shorty Gard, whose wife, Kathleen, played the piano at our church, used to cover their entire house with colored bulbs. It was a small house—in fact, I think it had formerly been a garage—but still. Sitting in the middle of a field the way it did, and shining out of the darkness, it was a little revelation. Three times a week during the holiday season my dad would say, "Let's go drive past Shorty's house," and we'd put on layers and layers of clothes and pile in the truck and drive a block down Jefferson Street, where the town ended and the country began.

Every year our church went caroling, and I would walk down the cold, dark streets next to my mom. The elm trees that lined Broad Street, meeting in the middle to form a canopy of leaves in the summer, were now just bare branches through which I could see the winter sky, sometimes bright with stars like ice, and sometimes dense and heavy with coming snow. It seemed there was someone home at every house, and as we stood in the street or on the porch, the men gathered in the back with their deep and smooth voices, the altos assembled behind my thin soprano, I would be washed in the heat that escaped through the front doors of all my fellow townspeople. Inside I would see the delicate decorations most people chose: candles, a wreath on the mantle, poinsettias on the windowsills. No one else went as far as Shorty; it was his role to please us so much. There was something perfect about the barest flicker of a candle in an upstairs window, there was something so lovely and restrained about the smallest changes. There was a suggestion in every house, just behind every door, that something miraculous was about to happen.

I WAS PROBABLY SIX YEARS OLD before I realized that most Christmas trees are green. Our tree, which my parents had for countless years, was made out of silver tinsel. When assembled, it looked like something a resourceful housewife might whip together out of old aluminum foil.

Now one would think that a tree made out of tinsel would last forever, that indeed, even if discarded it would have a twinkly landfill life of a few thousand years, but in fact, as the years passed the tree vanished before our eyes. Every year when we took it down we slid the fluffy silver arms into paper sleeves, to protect it in its box, and every year a few more tinsels fell off and were eaten by the dogs.

When my sister was sixteen she was finally, finally asked on a date by the cute Christian boy she had liked for years. He came to pick her up on a fairly balmy spring evening late in March. She brought him in the house to introduce him to my parents, and he was promptly greeted by the leprous family Christmas tree, all the lights flashing, all the ornaments dusty. Later in the evening, when he asked her why the tree was still up, she told him the truth: because Mom wanted to take a picture of it, and was just waiting to get some film.

FOR YEARS I was thrilled to receive one present from Santa, although when I was four I discovered that one present doesn't leave a child much to fall back on. That year my parents bought me a fluffy silver dog that had a music box inside. In the sequence of pictures taken just after we opened our gifts I am holding my dog close to me, obviously thrilled by it; in the next my sister is holding it and I am looking at it with my head cocked, confused; in the last the dog is completely gone and I am playing with the box it came in. I have just finished sneezing, and the fur of the dog, which came off in handfuls when touched, is lying all around me on the floor.

I was always grateful for my present because of something my dad told me. I asked him what he liked to play with when he was a little boy. He managed to look both wistful and brave.

"Oh, honey, we didn't really have any toys when I was a little boy." He went on to explain that when he was a child there was A Depression, which I understood perfectly well because sometimes my own mother didn't get dressed for days at a time, and would only sit in a corner of the couch reading science fiction novels and eating pork rinds.

"Well," I pursued, flabbergasted, "what about at Christmastime?"

He looked off into the distance, back into his long, long walk to school. "I was happy just to get an orange."

This was the most insane piece of news I had ever heard in my life. An orange was the *opposite* of a present; it was no different than saying, "I was happy just to get a baked potato," or "I was happy just to have a floor."

I felt a little shiver in my shoes. I would never be happy to get an orange. I didn't want an orange anywhere near me on Christmas morning—not the color or the smell or even anything that began with *o*.

I have since discovered that all men of a certain age tell this story, and they give themselves away by always using the same fruit. I have yet to meet the father who will look his child in the eye and say, "I was happy just to get some seedless grapes." But whatever the motive for this generational fiction, it works. So what if my stuffed dog molted and gave me an upper respiratory illness? At least Santa had remembered me, and at least I didn't have to eat it.

I HAD SOME DISAPPOINTMENTS with Santa, but not many. The only clear one I remember is the year I asked for a Skipper doll, who was an early, extra-perky friend of Barbie. Nobody had Barbies in Mooreland, and this could have posed a problem for the social Skipper, which might have been what Santa was thinking. Skipper was not the kind of girl to thrive in solitude. She wasn't doing much looking *inside*.

It's hard for me to say I didn't get Skipper, because I spent the whole month before Christmas fantasizing about her day and night: all the ways I would change her clothes, the apartment I would make for her out of a box, etc. She became so real to me that I hardly noticed her absence.

That year my only present was the game of Life, a darkly tedious enterprise whose sole saving grace is the excellent wheel one spins to decide one's pathetic fate. I continued spinning the wheel long after all the cars and plastic stick people were gone. The dogs became attracted to the small parts, and if history has taught us nothing else, it has taught us that one good swipe of a dog's tongue can take out fifteen sets of boy/girl twins, easy.

IT HAS BEEN MY tendency to say that Mooreland was behind the times, but it is probably more accurate to say that Mooreland was very confused about the times. For instance, in the 1970s people still referred to my mother as a Communist because she had a subscription to *The Atlantic Monthly,* which no one had ever heard of before. Ralph, our postmaster, refused to allow citizens to sub-

scribe to magazines of their own free will, insisting that they actually go to the drugstore, where we could pick them up in front of
our fellow townspeople. In this way he completely eliminated the
possibility of objectionable literature entering the town limits.

The only people current with the decade were Rose's parents,
William and Joyce. They were Catholic; they had traveled to
Acapulco; Joyce sometimes wore revealing, flowery dresses with
hats. The closest any other mother came to a hat was tying a ban-
danna around her head while sweeping out cobwebs. Joyce even
made her daughters wear panty hose to church, at a time when my
mother couldn't get me to wear socks, my argument being that
socks interfered with my need to dig at my welter of flea and mos-
quito bites. I'd never even *looked* squarely at a pair of panty hose.
They were terrifying things.

William and Joyce were ostracized most of the year for their
brazen ways, but they were the undisputed masters of Christmas.
My mother used to refer to them admiringly as the social liege
lords of our little province, their power crystallizing with their
Christmas Eve Party. To be invited was like grace.

I remember walking in the snow, under the muted light of the
streetlights, both of my parents dressed up in the best they had. We
walked past the Newmans' gas station; the Hickses' house; the
hardware store; Doc Austerman's veterinary clinic; the post office;
the home of Debbie Clancy, my sister's deaf friend; the North
Christian Church; the parsonage with the persimmon tree; and
there it was. A house I was in nearly as often as my own, but one
completely changed by lights and the imminent birth of the baby
Jesus, which would happen later, at the Midnight Mass Rose and
her family attended every year, whatever that was.

Inside it was all warmth and loud adult voices and *let me take your coats—Bob, the eggnog is in the dining room*. Rose and Maggie and their little brother, Patrick, were so jittery with excitement that Rose almost always got a big nosebleed. The table in the dining room was spread with such a feast my eye could barely hold it all. There were all kinds of unrecognizable foods in miniature, and a little gold umbrella-shaped thing that held gold swords for piercing the exotic foods. One crystal bowl held a gray paste that Rose swore to me was made of goose liver; she would not deny it even after I hit her for lying. For the rest of the evening I walked around giving myself the hookey-spooks by repeating the phrase "goose liver, goose liver, goose liver."

The eggnog was in a crystal bowl with matching crystal cups, and contained more alcohol than was permissible by Indiana law. Even before the adults started drinking there was much whispering and eyebrow-wagging about the fact of the eggnog, as if our parents were all back in high school watching the class clown spike the punch.

And then in the living room I saw the tree. It was enormous and sat directly on the floor, instead of on a table, as ours did. This was a thing with both depth and circumference, and it smelled of pine, rather than like the back of my parents' closet. Santa had not even come yet, but there were dozens of presents under the tree, including a basket of nuts with a nutcracker, and another with, oh, my God, oranges. I feared for my friends, and I also wanted to be them. I wanted such a tree in my house, and so many presents that they could simply be scattered about. It is an amazing moment, when one goes from being grateful for what one has to longing for what is impossible.

I would have stayed by the tree all night, but Rose wanted to go upstairs and begin playing Evil Queen, our favorite game, so I followed her reluctantly. I knew that sometime after her nosebleed we would all accidently fall asleep and I would wake up being carried home in the cold by my dad, who by that time would be emitting eggnog from his pores. We would get home, stoke the coal stove, and fall asleep on our couches and cots in the den. It was too cold to sleep next to the tree, but Santa came anyway. He was used to the cold.

THE YEAR I GOT THE LETTER I asked for a piano for Christmas. It was all I could think of: a piano, a piano, a piano. I had no idea what was compelling me in this desire, but it went straight to my heart, and I feared for myself if Santa didn't comply. This was way worse than the Skipper doll; it was worse, even, than the year I asked for and received my bicycle, which had seemed a miracle. I wanted the piano more than life itself, but I had also asked Santa for a doll with two buttons—one that made it be a real baby and one that turned it back into a doll. I was gambling: if I didn't get the piano at least I'd get the baby, and then I'd have something to live for.

My piano obsession was written in worry lines all over my parents' faces. I figured they were worried about where we'd put it. I assured them I'd be happy to give up my cot and sleep inside the piano if necessary, but they said nothing. I told them we could put it in the living room and I would cut all the fingertips out of my gloves and play it in there. Silence.

As Christmas Eve drew closer I also started to feel nervous. It seemed that nobody was holding out any hope for this one, even though I had wished it as hard as I could wish and had even begun praying to Santa instead of Jesus in Meeting on Sundays. After church, when everyone was gone, I took to sneaking up to the piano and quietly touching three keys, C, E, and G, stunned by my ability to make a little song. I couldn't imagine how I had figured such a difficult thing out all by myself—it was like magic, or fate.

On Christmas Eve, watching my parents get dressed for the party, I felt my stomach turn over with dread. There were a few things I had avoided facing that were now pressing down on me like snow clouds. 1) If Santa actually came down our chimney he would go straight into the coal stove, which had only a little round door in the front, not big enough for half of his fat, rosy face to get out. The larger ramifications of this I decided to avoid until some future date. 2) Even if Santa worked in such mysterious ways that he himself could get out of the red-hot coal stove, he could never get a piano through that hole, no matter how much I implored upon his mighty powers. 3) What if Santa was actually mad at me for asking him to carry such a thing as a piano all the way from the North Pole? What if flying it around caused one of the reindeer to founder, and Santa had to stop and shoot it in the head? How could I ever forgive myself?

As they dressed, Mom and Dad listened to Christmas carols on Dad's little brown radio. Just after "O Little Town of Bethlehem," the radio announcer came on to say that an unidentified flying object had been spotted somewhere over the east coast. Weather service radar was tracking the object, which seemed to be a large sleigh pulled by eight horselike creatures.

"Reindeer, you idiot," I muttered to the radio. I was annoyed that he had been spotted, because if The Radar People tracked him all the way to my house and something bad happened involving my piano, everyone would know.

I trudged despondently behind my parents all the way to Rose's house. My burden was already so heavy, and I hadn't even been faced with the heat and beauty and bounty that William and Joyce provided for their children. At one point, under the streetlight in front of the post office, my mom turned her head back toward me and said, "No matter how much it hurts, try to be gracious, sweetheart."

"Yes, ma'am," I said, thinking of all the times I had already tried, and how many gracious Christmases awaited me.

Rose met us at the door with one corner of a wet washcloth stuffed up her nose. Her wavy hair was so clean and shiny and black it looked blue in the Christmas lights. Her mother kept it cut very short and combed at all times. Her face was also shiny clean, and I noticed, after trying to measure how bad her nosebleed was by the condition of the washcloth, that she had on a pair of her mother's clip-on earrings. They weren't plastic, either, they were some kind of utterly precious metal, with real green stones in them. Probably emeralds. *Earrings.* I didn't dare look at her legs for panty hose fear.

She grabbed my hand before I could take off my coat and hat. "Come quick! You've got to see the early Christmas presents we got!"

We stopped at the Christmas tree, where she showed me a Santa about a foot tall, made out of what I now know was white chocolate. I assumed it was the biggest bar of soap in the world. Rose took a bite off the tip of his hat, which I took to be some

Catholic thing, then offered it to me, but I refused, holding up my hands and backing up at the same time. It hadn't been so long since I'd had some soap to eat at my own house, after telling my mother to go to hell.

The real present was up in her room, she said, dragging me up the stairs. She led me into her room with her hands over my eyes, positioned me, then pulled them away, shouting, "Okay, look!"

It was a piano. Well, not exactly a piano, more like an organ. And not like a church organ, this was a little organ that sat on the floor. And it didn't have a full keyboard, just two octaves and buttons you pushed for the chords, but it might as well have been a piano.

I wondered if it would still work if I threw up on it. I wondered what would happen to the beautiful little white keys if I picked Rose up and threw her down on it, repeatedly. I wondered what on earth I was supposed to do with myself now.

"And look! It came with a book of Christmas songs! I can't play any of them yet, but I bet you could, and then we could sing them. Here, see, you just play the notes by the number written right here with this hand, and then with the other hand you press the chord button. You try."

I was nodding, yeah, yeah, it was perfectly clear what I was supposed to do, and then I was sitting on the floor with my legs crossed Indian-style playing "O Come, All Ye Faithful," except that this book had both the English and the Latin, which Rose already knew and chose to sing. *Latin.* I'd never heard such a thing in my life. It sounded utterly Catholic. It sounded incredibly beautiful and strange, like soap you'd want to eat. When we reached the end of the song I had tears in my eyes, but I would have stuck an ice pick in my own eardrum before I would have cried in front of Rose and Maggie.

I went downstairs to the bathroom, where there were still spatters of blood on the sink and mirror from Rose's big nose problem. I looked in the mirror at my saddest self; my hair was winging up all over my head, and I had a smear of something charcoaly across one cheek. Part of my shirt collar was tucked under and I had a gray ring around my neck, because I refused to allow it to be washed, on principle. Some of my permanent teeth hadn't come in yet, but the two front ones had come in overlapped, and big as horse's teeth. Who would give something so fine as a miniature piano to someone like me? What on earth had I ever done to deserve it?

Outside the bathroom door I could hear my parents conferring. It had begun to snow quite hard, and my dad was saying he thought he ought to go home and get the truck, so that Mom and I wouldn't have to trudge home later. I waited until he was gone and then stepped out of the bathroom, where my mom was standing silently waiting for me.

I slammed my head into her warm, soft shoulder, choking back a sob.

"They gave her a *piano*," I said, miserably.

"I know."

"How could they?!" I nearly cried. William and Joyce didn't love me, not like Julie's parents did, but I thought they cared a little bit.

"I'm sure they didn't mean to hurt your feelings," she said, trying fruitlessly to smooth down my wicked hair.

"That's the same thing you said when my teachers *spanked* me, like it was an accident." My mom could get me so indignant.

"Well, that was different, I'll admit. But I think what you'll discover more and more as you get older is that most people aren't thinking about you at all."

She kissed me on top of the head and sent me back upstairs. We sang some more carols, Rose chased me with goose liver for a while, then we settled down to Evil Queen. Not long into it Rose and Maggie fell asleep, but I never did. I was nearly despondent by the time we put our coats on to leave.

As we got into Dad's warm truck my parents said nothing about my despair, and I swore to myself I would never comment on it again, either. So my best friend got the one thing I wanted most, the one thing I would never have? So what if when she woke up in the morning there would be presents spread so far out across the living room floor the children would have to begin opening presents in the hallway? What was all this to me?

Our house looked cold; the lights from the tinsel tree feeble. In the living room we could see our breath. I took off my coat and boots and started to turn left to go straight into the warm den, but my dad stopped me and eased me deeper into the living room.

And there, in front of our sweet little tree, stood a piano. Not a piano, exactly, more like an organ. Not a church-size organ, but one much, much bigger than Rose's. It stood on *legs*. It had its own *bench*. It had probably four octaves, and three music books. And propped up on the music stand was a letter, written in script so ancient it wobbled, big, loopy handwriting that could only come from a very shy, very strange man:

Dear Child,

I hope you don't mind that I delivered this a day early, but I thought you might like to have it tonight. I'm sorry I can't also bring you the doll, but to be honest, no one has ever before made such a request. My elves are working on it, but it might be a long time before we get it just right.

Thank you for not losing faith. Thank you for being so brave tonight.

Love,
Santa

The author gratefully acknowledges the kindness and support of the following people: Tom Koontz, Tom Mullen, the faculty, staff, and students of the Earlham School of Religion. My first family: Bob Jarvis, Delonda Hartmann, Melinda Frame, Daniel Jarvis. My other families: the Pitchers, the Newmans, the Hickses, and all the good people of the Mooreland Friends Church. Beth Pitcher Dalton. Julie Newman Attaway. Loretta Orion. Will and Dorothy Kennedy. Carolyn Chute and Pamela de Marris. Ben Kimmel, who makes all things possible. My daughter, Katie, and my son, Obadiah. Don and Meg Kimmel. Dick and Anna Boykin, who gave me a computer. Tom and Noelle Milam. Lawrence Naumoff and Marianne Gingher.

My agent, Stella Connell, and my editor, Amy Scheibe. Paula Press and John Rosenthal. Lee Smith. And John Svara, guardian angel of every word.

A GUIDE FOR
READING GROUPS
(or for *Anyone Who Wants to Ponder Zippy Further*)

Whisking us to a simpler time and a much, much simpler place, *A Girl Named Zippy* provides a refreshing escape from twenty-first-century woes. If your reading group has decided to treat itself to a Mooreland sojourn, you'll discover that there's plenty to say about the town's most imaginative little girl (even if she did remain speechless until age three). We hope that the following questions will enhance your discussion, spotlight memorable passages, and make your reading experience even livelier. For information about other Broadway Books reading group guides, visit us at www. broadwaybooks.com.

1. Zippy's numerous pets include Sam the Pig, Speckles the Chicken, the dogs Kai and Tiger, a pony named Tim, the cats PeeDink and Smokey, and Skippy the Hamster. How does Haven Kimmel develop the animals as sympathetic characters or villains (such as Chanticleer, the abusive rooster)? How does a child's

bond with animals differ from that of an adult? Which of Zippy's pet stories was the most memorable for you? Discuss the significant animals of your own childhood.

2. At first glance, *A Girl Named Zippy* appears to be a collection of assorted scenes, almost like a scrapbook. Yet the chapters unfold as if they were part of a novel. What themes thread their way through the work as a whole? What recurring predicaments are resolved as Zippy gets older?

3. Haven Kimmel introduces us to a slew of eccentric Mooreland residents, from the grumpy drugstore owner to the postman who delivers only the mail he approves of. How do various communities—big cities and small towns alike—define eccentricity? Were Mooreland's attempts at clean living successful? How does Mooreland compare to your town?

4. The introductory quote from Emerson asks, "Is there no event . . . which shall not, sooner or later, lose its adhesive, inert form?" Which portions of *A Girl Named Zippy* do you perceive as being precisely accurate, and which ones seem slightly embellished by the process Emerson calls "soaring from our body into the empyrean"?

5. Consider Zippy's family: her gun-toting but sensitive dad, bookish mother, adored big brother, and mercurial big sister. In what ways is the Jarvis family dynamic both typical and unusual?

6. Does Haven Kimmel seem to approve or disapprove of her upbringing?

7. Zippy often discusses religion. How does her mother's Quaker community differ from her father's "church in the woods"? Is he really as godless as his wife thinks he is?

8. Numerous memoirs have been published that expose deeply painful childhoods. Haven Kimmel alludes to a few dark aspects of life in Mooreland, such as poverty, a lecherous teacher, and her father's gambling problem. How do Zippy's coping skills compare to those of other children you've read about?

9. The chapter entitled "The World of Ideas" introduces us to Zippy's maternal grandmother, described as "a moneyed old woman in a small, depressed city." What insight does this section give us into Zippy's mother, who was raised in an environment that was very different from Zippy's?

10. How was Zippy changed by her friendship with Dana, whose parents worked in a factory, were atheists, and seemed uninterested in their child?

11. A few aspects of Zippy's childhood would be hard to find in today's households. Which of her recollections best represent the late 1960s and early 1970s?

12. Zippy had an unusual bond with Julie, her snaggletoothed friend. How do you suppose Zippy was able to interpret Julie's silence, even over the phone? Why did Julie hit Zippy three times in the chapter of the same name?

13. Petey was Zippy's nemesis, abusing animals and even raising a carnivorous rabbit. Discuss the grade-school bullies in your past. What sort of adults did they become?

14. What is it about Haven Kimmel's tone that makes even everyday events seem compelling? How does she balance humor and poignancy?

15. Where the Jarvises poor?

16. In light of the book's beginning, what is the significance of the story in the final chapter, in which Zippy receives a piano from Santa? What do the closing sentences "Thank you for not losing faith" and "Thank you for being so brave tonight" reveal about Zippy and her parents?

John Rosenthal

Haven Kimmel is the author of the novel *The Solace of Leaving Early*. She studied English and creative writing at Ball State University and North Carolina State University and attended seminary at the Earlham School of Religion. She lives in Durham, North Carolina.